SHAMBHALA DRAGON EDITIONS

The dragon is an age-old symbol of the highest spiritual essence, embodying wisdom, strength, and the divine power of transformation. In this spirit, Shambhala Dragon Editions offers a treasury of readings in the sacred knowledge of Asia. In presenting the works of authors both ancient and modern, we seek to make these teachings accessible to lovers of wisdom everywhere.

The

FIVE
HOUSES
of ZEN

Thomas Cleary

SHAMBHALA
Boston & London
1997

SHAMBHALA PUBLICATIONS, INC.
Horticultural Hall
300 Massachusetts Avenue
Boston, Massachusetts 02115
www.shambhala.com

Printed in the United States of America
Distributed in the United States by Random House, Inc.,
and in Canada by Random House of Canada Ltd

Library of Congress Cataloging-in-Publication Data
The five houses of Zen/Thomas Cleary.—
   p. cm.—(Shambhala dragon editions)
    ISBN 1-57062-292-2 (alk. paper)
  1. Zen Buddhism—China. 2. Zen Buddhism—
Quotations, maxims, etc. 3. Priests, Zen—China.
     I. Cleary, Thomas F., 1949– .
         II. Series.
BQ9262.9.C5F8   1996   96-44399
294.3′927′0951—dc21   CIP

BVG 01

Contents

v

CONTENTS

The House of Yun-men

The House of Fa-yen

Introduction

WHEN BUDDHISM TOOK ROOT in China after the end of the Han dynasty (206 BCE–219 CE), it triggered the release of enormous waves of creative energy from a people who had been spiritually imprisoned for centuries. For four hundred years the mainstream Chinese culture had been kept within the suffocating confines of narrow-minded Confucian orthodoxy, imposed by the ruling house of Han as part of its handle on political power.

Not the least of the effects of Buddhism on China was the development of Taoism, China's native spiritual tradition, in highly elaborated religious and literary formats emulating the extraordinarily rich intellectual and aesthetic expressiveness of Buddhism. Yet even with the rapid expansion of Taoism, the more internationalized China of the post-Han centuries found Buddhist teachings immensely attractive, and the two religions grew side by side in the lively syncretic culture evolving in the new China.

While Buddhist literature and learning expanded the minds of the Chinese intelligentsia, Buddhist adepts took an active role in the resettlement and reconstruction of war-torn territories in the aftermath of the breakup of the old order. As relatively local and short-lived dynasties rose and fell over the following centuries, eventually Chinese warlords emulated their central Asian counterparts and began adopting Buddhism as a kind of state religion.

In contrast to Confucianism, Buddhism was an international religion, without ethnic or cultural bias. Like Druidism in pre-Roman Europe, in addition to being a repository of many kinds of knowledge, Buddhism served as a medium for international cultural and diplomatic exchange throughout most of Asia, even—perhaps especially—in times when warfare ravaged the world at large.

There was, naturally, a drawback to the flourishing of Buddhist religion in China. As a Zen saying goes, "One gain, one loss." Having become well established, well funded, and well thought of, Buddhism came to attract many idlers and many greedy and ambitious poseurs. Some sought material support, some sought intellectual diversion, some sought political power. The abundance of ritual, literature, and organizational methods that Buddhism offered was intoxicating to many Chinese aristocrats and warlords.

A result of the bewildering volume and variety of Buddhist literature pouring into China from south and central Asia was the development of schools of Chinese Buddhism based either on certain important texts or on certain arrangements of the whole body of canonical teachings. This process was already beginning by the early fifth century, and by the end of the sixth century the first syncretic school, T'ien-t'ai, had absorbed a number of earlier schools that had been more limited in scope.

The next three centuries saw the most distinctive and most sophisticated stage of evolution, not only of Chinese Buddhism but of Chinese culture as a whole. This was the age of the T'ang dynasty (619–906), the zenith of the civilization and the greatest expression of its complex genius.

T'ang culture was highly stimulated by the vigorous policies of the Empress Wu Tse-t'ien (r. 684–701), a highly accomplished individual who promoted Confucianism, Taoism, and Buddhism to enrich the spiritual resources of the entire civilization. Discussion and debate among the three ways of thought were promoted, in order to discourage complacency under state sponsorship and bring out the best in each of the philosophies.

It was during the T'ang dynasty that the Buddhist schools of Pure Land, T'ien-t'ai, Hua-yen, Chen-yen (Mantra) and Ch'an (Zen) were given their definitive expression by the great masters of the age. The Pure Land school was taken to new heights of mystic experience by the ecstatic writings of Shan-tao; the T'ien-t'ai meditation exercises were elaborately facilitated in the technical commentaries of Chan-jan; the Hua-yen universe was brilliantly illuminated in the essays of Fa-hsiang; the secrets of Tantric Buddhism were encapsulated in the esoteric art of Hui-kuo; and the inner mind of Ch'an or Zen Buddhism was straightforwardly revealed in the lectures of Hui-neng.

Certain hallmarks distinguished Zen from other schools. One of the most evident of these is the greater diversity of Zen expression, which is rooted in the fact that classical Zen was stricter in observance of the Mahayana Buddhist axiom that particular systems cannot be fixed as universal prescriptions for everyone's enlightenment. While Zen and other schools of Buddhism share a vast range of teachings, their modes and methods of expedient selection, organization, and presentation differ greatly.

To be practical, approaches and methods have to be adjusted to the needs and capacities of communities and individuals. This is not a Zen idea but is basic to Buddhism as a whole. Buddhist principles and practices vary over a wide spectrum for this reason, and their breadth and flexibility were also reflected in the custom of original Zen teachers to encourage and stimulate direct individual experience and avoid dogmatic cliché.

In accord with its pragmatic nature, Zen interpretation of

Buddhist scripture dropped mythological thinking in favor of analogical thinking. Buddhist scriptures were not treated by Zen adepts as holy writ that was necessarily regarded as literally true, but as compendia of potentially useful ideas, outlooks, and exercises, commonly couched in sometimes dazzling symbolic language. Insisting on understanding the scriptures in practical terms, not just reciting them piously, the leading masters of Zen interpreted Buddhist symbolism by a special kind of structural analysis based on aspects and phases of Buddhist experiences of awakening and awareness. This discipline was also applied to the growing body of special Zen lore, particularly stories and poems.

Because of its nature and history, there is no fixed curriculum and no standard textbook of genuine classical Zen. Most of the material that would be required for a real history of Zen does not actually exist. This is part of the original teaching of Zen, which has to be experienced personally to be understood and whose masters consequently spoke to the needs of others and did not talk much about themselves.

Although there is no fixed canon as such in Zen, some writings and remnants of classical teachings have been preserved. Parts of this lore were used in various ways from time to time in Zen revivals, and an immense secondary literature of interpretation and elaboration also came into being, parts of which were picked up in yet later movements and revivals. This eventually resulted in extremely convoluted, indeed involuted, literary mannerisms, which contributed to the decline and demise of experiential illuminist Zen.

Within the vast body of recognized Zen literature emanating from countless teachers and schools appearing and disappearing over the centuries, the work that stands out preeminently as the mother lode of classical examples of Zen is that which is associated with the so-called Five Houses of Zen. Historically represented by several groups of outstanding Zen teachers, the Five Houses arose in China during the ninth and tenth centuries.

The Five Houses were not sects or schools, but later they came to be thought of that way. Although the grand masters of the Five Houses were eminent teachers, and the theoretical concept of the Houses seems to center around their teachings, in fact virtually nothing is known of the inner or outer lives of these individuals, and no organizations can actually be traced to them. In short, the original Houses were not institutionalized, their teachings were not dogmatized, and their guides and exemplars were not idolized.

The Five Houses of Classical Zen, in order of historical emergence, were the Kuei-Yang, named after the masters Kuei-shan Ling-yu (771–854) and Yang-shan Hui-chi (813–890); the Lin-chi, named after the master Lin-chi I-hsuan (d. 866); the Ts'ao-Tung, named after the masters Tung-shan Liang-chieh (807–869) and Ts'ao-shan Pen-chi (840–901); the Yun-men, named after the master Yun-men Wen-yen (d. 949); and the Fa-yen, named after the master Fa-yen Wen-i (885–958).

The present collection of teachings from the Five Houses of Zen begins with sayings of Pai-chang Huai-hai (720–814), who was the teacher of Kuei-shan Ling-yu of the House of Kuei-Yang. Also a direct forerunner of the House of Lin-chi, Pai-chang is credited with the early Zen rule "A day without work, a day without food," which fostered independence from secular patronage. Pai-chang's sayings are strongly infused with scriptural Buddhist teachings, and this characteristic also marks the subsequent works of the masters of the Kuei-Yang and Lin-chi Houses.

Following Pai-chang's sayings are extracts from the *Admonitions* of Kuei-shan, one of the earliest Zen writings. During the Sung dynasty (960–1278), this work was incorporated into a popular primer of Buddhism and subsequently was made the object of much study and commentary. Orally transmitted sayings of Kuei-shan and his successor Yang-shan appear in many classical anthologies of Zen works, and numerous dialogues between them are used as examples in major collections of teaching stories.

Relatively little is known or recorded of later masters of the House of Kuei-Yang, which returned to quiescence after a few generations. An exception to this is found in a rare record of the work of Sun-chi, a successor of Yang-shan, who came from Korea and whose sayings are found only in the *Annals of the Halls of the Ancestors*, an early Zen collection lost in China but preserved (and apparently augmented) in Korea.

This material is particularly valuable in that it contains the most extensive and most clearly explained usages of circular symbols, for which the House of Kuei-Yang is said to have been famous. Yang-shan is supposed to have inherited a unique book of symbols from an ancient master. To avoid attachment to the concrete, Yang-shan burned this book but later made a copy from memory to return to the master from whom he received it. Nothing more is known of this system, except for fragments appearing here and there. Sun-chi's explanations clarify the mystery of the circular symbols to some degree, particularly in demonstrating the connection between scriptural Buddhism and Zen.

After the Kuei-Yang, the next of the Five Houses of Zen was the Lin-chi. The selection of materials presented here begins with extracts from *Essential Method of Transmission of Mind* by Huang-po (d. 850), who was the Zen teacher of Lin-chi, after whom the House is named. Huang-po is said to have been enlightened by nature, but he is also considered a Zen successor of the great Pai-chang.

Huang-po's sayings are followed by excerpts from the *Lin-chi Lu*, or "Record of Lin-chi," one of the most extensive collections of lectures and dialogues of an individual teacher to be made during the classical period of Zen. Reflecting the spirit of Pai-chang and Huang-po in his teaching, Lin-chi further refined some of their formal didactic constructs and also perfected the use of shock techniques to stimulate direct perceptual breakthrough outside of conventional thought patterns.

The Lin-chi House of Zen declined almost immediately and was nearly extinct after the fourth generation. It was revived by a sixth-generation master who studied with more than seventy teachers of Zen, including representatives of all the existing Houses as well as other Zen lineages. This revival of Lin-chi Zen was brought to its greatest level of sophistication in the tenth generation by the Zen master Yuan-wu (1063–1135), whose famous *Essentials of Mind* also became a Zen classic. Extracts of this work are presented here.

The Ts'ao-Tung House of Zen arose at more or less the same time as the Kuei-Yang and Lin-chi. The records of the masters of this House were scattered, and little remains but some dialogues and a few compositions attributed to Tung-shan and Ts'ao-shan. The selection presented here begins with sayings of Tung-shan's predecessors Yao-shan (745–828) and Yun-yen (781–841). The teaching embodied in Tung-shan's famed *Song of Focusing the Precious Mirror*, given here in translation, is said to have originated with Yao-shan and been transmitted to Tung-shan by Yun-yen.

The House of Ts'ao-Tung is particularly known for the teaching device of the Five Ranks, said to have been extracted from Yao-shan's teaching by Tung-shan and refined by his successor Ts'ao-shan. The present collection includes Ts'ao-shan's most remarkable exposition of this device, which primarily illustrates the integration of absolute and relative perspectives in Zen experience, extending its use to structural analysis of Zen sayings and stories to define the states and stages of realization they represent.

The Ts'ao-Tung school died out after the passing of the last of the sixth-generation masters but was revived by a seventh-generation master of the House of Lin-chi, who had been entrusted with the Ts'ao-Tung teaching methods by the last living master. A subsequent revival of the Ts'ao-Tung House of Zen ultimately climaxed in the teachings of Hung-chih (1091–1157), who turned out to be one of the greatest Zen writers of all time, in both poetry and prose. Selections from Hung-chih's remarkable writings cap this chapter on the Ts'ao-Tung House of Zen.

The fourth of the Five Houses is named after Yun-men, who studied with a disciple of Huang-po and attained enlightenment before meeting Hsueh-feng, who is traditionally regarded as his main Zen teacher. Hsueh-feng himself studied with Tung-shan of the House of Ts'ao-Tung Zen, and Yun-men later associated with Tung-shan's successor Ts'ao-shan. After completing his studies with Hsueh-feng, Yun-men also spent time with a successor of Kuei-shan of the House of Kuei-Yang Zen. Thus the Yun-men House of Zen had spiritual connections with each of the older Houses.

The selection of materials on Yun-men Zen presented here begins with sayings of Hsueh-feng (822–908), who was the teacher of Yun-men and of many other distinguished Zen masters of the age. Hsueh-feng attained his first Zen realization at the age of eighteen, but he did not reach complete Zen enlightenment until he was forty-five and is traditionally held up as a prime illustration of the proverb, "A good vessel takes a long time to complete." He subsequently attracted many followers and is said to have had fifteen hundred disciples. By the time he died, he had more than fifty enlightened successors already teaching Zen.

Yun-men, after whom the House is named, was one of the

most brilliant and abstruse of all the classical masters. His talks include numerous examples of quotations and variations of existing Zen lore, and meditation on Zen stories and sayings was clearly one of the methods of his school. Tradition has it, nevertheless, that Yun-men forbade his followers to record his own words, so that they could not memorize sayings at the expense of direct experience of reality. The record we nonetheless have of Yun-men, more extensive than that of other original masters of the Five Houses, is said to have been surreptitiously written down by a longtime disciple on a robe made of paper. Such robes were sometimes worn by monks as an exercise in remembrance of the perishability of things. This anthology presents several of Yun-men's lectures, in which he gives orientation for Zen studies in relatively straightforward terms.

Yun-men had sixty-one enlightened disciples, but little is known of most of them. In the next generation, however, a successor of one of his disciples emerged as a leading writer and intellectual of his time as well as a distinguished Zen master. This was the great master Ming-chiao (1008–1072), who wrote extensively on secular subjects as well as religious and spiritual themes. Ming-chiao had many contacts among the Confucian intelligentsia, and he played a powerful role in the Zen influence on the emergence and development of Sung dynasty neo-Confucianism. Several of Ming-chiao's lucid essays on psychology and spirituality are presented here in the materials on the Yun-men House of Zen.

In the next, fourth, generation of this Zen House, another giant arose, the eminent Hsueh-tou, who was also a great writer and an outstanding poet. Traditionally regarded as the reviver of the House of Yun-men, Hsueh-tou is particularly famous as the author of the poetic commentaries on Zen stories of the classic collection *Blue Cliff Record.* Another collection of poetry is also attributed to Hsueh-tou, as well as an anthology of Zen

stories with his own prose comments, the *Cascade Collection*, selections of which are presented here to cap the section on Yun-
men Zen.

The last of the Five Houses of Zen was the Fa-yen. One of
the earliest collections of classical Zen lore refers to this House
as a revival of the Zen school of Hsuan-sha (835–908), one of
the most redoubtable masters of the T'ang dynasty. Originally
a fisherman, Hsuan-sha became an apprentice and colleague of
the great Zen master Hsueh-feng, already mentioned as the
forerunner of the Yun-men House.

The selection of materials presented here on the Fa-yen
House of Zen begins with sayings of Hsuan-sha and his successor Kuei-ch'en, who was the teacher of Zen master Fa-yen. This
is followed by the complete text of Fa-yen's classic composition
Ten Guidelines for Zen Schools, in which the great master—who
is said to have had a thousand disciples and more than sixty
enlightened successors—analyzes the deterioration of contem-
porary Zen teaching and practice vis-à-vis the fundamental
principles and original ideals of Zen.

Among Fa-yen's many spiritual heirs were numerous distinguished Zen masters, including a National Teacher of Koryo,
unified Korea, where this House was to have a great impact.
Another of his outstanding successors, a National Teacher of the
Latter Han dynasty in post-T'ang China, was instrumental in
the restoration and revival of the T'ien-t'ai school of Buddhism,
one of the mother houses of ancient Zen. This master was in
turn succeeded by the illustrious Yung-ming Yen-shou (905–
976), who is also considered a patriarch of Pure Land Buddhism.

Yen-shou revitalized the study of pan-Buddhism in the Zen
context and the study of Zen in the pan-Buddhism context. He
was probably the most prolific Zen author of all time, especially
noted for his hundred-volume compendium *Source Mirror Record*, in which he synthesizes the whole range of exoteric Bud-

dhist doctrine, quoting extensively from more than three hundred classical sources.

This anthology of materials from the Five Houses of Zen closes with two selections from the work of Yen-shou of the House of Fa-yen. First is a summary critique of more than one hundred cultic deviations of Zen, following on the work of Fa-yen and others along these lines. This is followed by an instructive work on balancing the two basic aspects of meditation, commonly referred to as cessation and contemplation (or stopping and seeing) in the context of causative practice, and as concentration and insight (or stability and wisdom) in the context of effective realization. This is one of the most valuable guides to Zen meditation to be found among the literature of the Five Houses.

The House of
KUEI-YANG

PAI-CHANG

Sayings

It is necessary to distinguish language referring to absolute truth from language referring to relative truth. It is necessary to distinguish general statements from particular statements. It is necessary to distinguish the language of a complete teaching from the language of an incomplete teaching.

The complete teaching deals with purity; the incomplete teaching deals with impurity. The incomplete teaching explains the defilement in impure things in order to eliminate the profane; the complete teaching explains the defilement in pure things in order to eliminate the sacred.

Before Buddha had expounded the elementary teachings, people had no vision, so they needed someone to refine them. If you are speaking to unhearing worldlings, you need to teach them to get over their attachments, live a disciplined life, practice meditation, and develop insight. But it is not appropriate to speak in this way to people beyond measure.

People in the process of self-purification have already willingly accepted discipline in full. Theirs is the power of discipline, concentration, and insight; therefore to preach to them in this way is called speaking at the wrong time, because it is not appropriate to the occasion. It is also called suggestive talk.

People in the process of purification must be told of the defilement in pure things. They must be taught to detach from all things, existent or nonexistent. They must be taught to detach from all cultivation and experience and even to detach from detachment.

The process of purification is to strip away influences of habit. If people in the process of purification cannot get rid of the diseases of greed and hatred, they are also unhearing worldlings and still have to be taught to practice meditation and cultivate insight.

The two lesser vehicles put an end to the diseases of greed and hatred, removing them completely, yet dwell in desirelessness and consider that correct. This is the formless realm; this is obstructing the light of complete enlightenment, shedding the blood of Buddha. Here too it is still necessary to practice meditation and develop insight further.

You have to distinguish references to purity and impurity. There are many names for impure things—greed, hatred, infatuation, and so on. There are also many names for pure things—enlightenment, nirvana, liberation, and so on. Yet even in the very midst of these twin streams, purity and impurity—in the midst of standards of profanity and holiness, in the midst of forms, sounds, smells, tastes, feelings, and things, in the midst of worldly things and transmundane phenomena—the immediate mirroring awareness should not get fixated on anything at all.

Once you are free of obsession and fixation, if you abide in non-attachment and consider that correct, this is the elementary good. This is abiding in the subdued mind. This is what a disciple is. You are attached to the means and will not let go of it. This is the way of the two lesser vehicles. This is a result of meditation.

Once you are no longer grasping, and yet do not dwell in nonattachment either, this is the intermediate good. This is the Half Word Teaching. This is still the formless realm; although you avoid being trapped in the way of the two lesser vehicles and avoid being trapped by bedevilment, this is still a meditation sickness. This is the bondage of enlightening beings.

Once you no longer dwell in nonattachment and do not even make an understanding of nonabiding, this is the final good. This is the Full Word Teaching. You avoid being trapped in the formless realm, avoid being trapped in meditation sickness, avoid being trapped in the way of enlightening beings, and avoid being trapped by bedevilment.

Because of barriers of knowledge, barriers of state, and barriers of action, seeing your own buddha nature is like seeing color at night. As it is said, in the stage of buddhahood, two kinds of ignorance are stopped: the ignorance of subtle knowledge and the ignorance of extremely subtle knowledge.

If you can pass through the three phases of beginning, intermediate, and final goodness, you will not be constrained by them. Buddhist teachings liken this to a deer leaping three times to get out of a net. Then you are called an enlightened one beyond confinement; nothing can capture or bind you. You are one of the buddhas succeeding to the Lamp Buddha. This is the supreme vehicle, the highest knowledge; this is standing on the

Way of enlightenment. You are now a buddha, with enlightened nature; you are a guide, able to employ an unobstructed influence. This is unimpeded illumination.

After enlightenment, you will be able to use causality of virtue and knowledge freely; this is building a car to carry causality. In life, you are not stayed by life; in death, you are not obstructed by death. Even though you are within the clusters of mental and physical elements, it is as if a door had opened up, so you are not inhibited by these clusters of mental and physical elements. You are free to leave or to remain, going out and entering without difficulty. If you can be like this, there is no question of stages or steps, of superior or inferior; everything, even down to the bodies of ants, is all the land of pure marvel. It is inconceivable.

The foregoing is still just talk for the purpose of untying bonds. As scripture says, "They themselves are whole; don't injure them." Even terms like *Buddha* and *enlightening beings* are injuries. As long as you speak of anything at all, whether it exists or not, it is all injury. "Whether it exists or not" refers to all things.

Enlightening beings of the tenth stage are still in the river of impure streams; they create a teaching of a pure stream, defining characteristics of purity and explaining the afflictions of impurity.

In ancient times, the ten great disciples of Buddha all had their individuality and characteristic condition; one by one they had their errors explained away by the Guide. In the four stages of meditation and eight concentrations, even the likes of saints dwell in absorption for as long as eighty thousand eons; clinging dependently to what they practice, they are intoxicated by the wine of pure things.

Therefore, disciples may hear the teaching of the Enlightened One but are not able to conceive the spirit of the supreme Way. That is why it is said that people who cut off roots of goodness have no buddha nature. A scripture says this is called the deep pit of liberation, a fearsome place; if the mind retreats for an instant, it goes to hell like an arrow shot.

We cannot speak only in terms of retreating or not retreating, since supernal enlightening beings like Manjushri, Avalokiteshvara, and Mahasthamaprapta come back to the stage of stream-entering, mingling with various kinds of people in order to guide them. We cannot say that they have retreated or regressed; all we can say at such times is that they have entered the stream.

As long as the immediate mirroring awareness is not concerned by anything at all, whether it exists or not, and can pass through the three stages and all things, pleasant or unpleasant, then even if you hear of a hundred, a thousand, or even a hundred million buddhas appearing in the world, it is as if you had not heard. And yet you do not dwell in not hearing, and you do not make an understanding of nondwelling. Then you cannot be said to retreat; measurements and calculations do not apply to you. This is what is meant by the saying that Buddha is always in the world without being habituated to things of the world.

To say the Buddha turns the Wheel of the Teaching and then retreats is to slander the Enlightened One, the Teaching, and the Community. To say the Buddha does not turn the Wheel of the Teaching and does not retreat is also to slander the Enlightened One, the Teaching, and the Community. As Seng Chao wrote, "The Way of enlightenment cannot be measured; it is so high that there is nothing above it, so vast that it cannot be limited, so profound that it is bottomless, so deep that it cannot be fathomed. Even to speak of it is like setting up a target, inviting an arrow."

When we speak of mirroring awareness, even this is not really right. Discern the pure by way of the impure. If you say the immediate mirroring awareness is right, or else that there is something beyond mirroring awareness, this is all delusion. If you keep dwelling in immediate mirroring awareness, this is also tantamount to delusion; this is what is called the mistake of naturalism.

If you say immediate mirroring awareness is your own Buddha, these are words of measurement, words of calculation; they are like the crying of a jackal. This is being stuck at the gate, like being stuck in glue.

Originally you did not acknowledge that innate knowing and awareness are your own Buddha, and so you went running elsewhere to seek Buddha. Therefore you needed a teacher to tell you about innate knowing and awareness, as a medicine to cure this disease of frantic outward seeking.

Once you no longer seek outwardly, this disease is cured, and it is necessary to remove the medicine. If you cling fixedly to innate knowing awareness, this is a Zen sickness, characteristic of a fanatical follower. It is like water turned to ice: all the ice is water, but it cannot be used to quench thirst. This is a mortal illness, before which ordinary physicians are helpless.

There has never been such a thing as "Buddha," so do not understand it as Buddha. "Buddha" is a medicine for emotional people; if you have no disease, you should not take medicine. When medicine and disease are both dissolved, it is like pure water; buddhahood is like a sweet herb mixed in the water, or like honey mixed in the water, most sweet and delicious. And yet the pure water itself is not affected.

It is not that there is nothing there, because it has always been there. This truth is originally present in everyone. All the buddhas and enlightening beings may be called people pointing out a treasure. Fundamentally, it is not a thing; you don't need to know or understand it; you don't need to affirm or deny it. Just stop dualism; stop suppositions of being and nonbeing, of neither being nor nonbeing.

When there are no traces of either extreme, then there is neither lack nor sufficiency; this is not profane or holy, not light or dark. This is not having knowledge, yet it is not lacking knowledge. It is not bondage and not liberation. It is not any name or category at all. Why is this not true speech? How can you carve and polish emptiness to make an image of Buddha? How can you say that emptiness is blue, yellow, red, or white?

It is said, "Reality has no comparison, because there is nothing to which it may be likened; the body of reality is not constructed and does not fall within the scope of any category." That is why it is said, "The reality of the enlightened is nameless and cannot be expressed in speech; it is impossible to tarry in the empty door of truth as it really is." Just as insects can alight anywhere but on the flames of a fire, the minds of emotional people can form relations to anything except transcendent insight.

When you visit teachers, seeking some knowledge or understanding, this is the demon of teachers, because it gives rise to talk and opinion.

If you take the four universal vows, promising to rescue all living beings before attaining buddhahood yourself, this is the demon of the knowledge of the way of enlightening beings, because the vow is never given up.

If you fast and discipline yourself, practice meditation, and cultivate insight, these are afflicted virtues. Even if you manifest attainment of complete, perfect enlightenment and rescue innumerable people, enabling them to attain individual enlightenment, this is the demon of virtues, since it arouses greed and attachment.

If you are completely undefiled by greed in the midst of all things, so that your aware essence exists alone, dwelling in extremely deep absorption without ever rising or progressing further, this is the demon of concentration, because you will be permanently addicted to enjoying it until you reach ultimate extinction, desireless, quiescent, and still. This is still demon work.

If your insight cannot shed so many demon webs, then even if you can understand a hundred books of knowledge, all of it is dregs of hell. If you seek to be like Buddha, there is no way for you to be so.

Now when you hear me tell you not to be attached to anything at all, whether good or bad, existent or nonexistent, you immediately take that to be falling into a void. You don't realize that abandoning the root to pursue the branches is falling into a void. Seeking buddhahood, seeking enlightenment, seeking anything at all, whether it exists or not, is abandoning the root to pursue the branches.

For now, eat simple food to sustain life, wear old clothing to keep off the cold, and when thirsty scoop up water to drink. Beyond this, if you harbor no thought of concern with anything at all, whether it is there or not, then you will in time have your share of ease and clarity.

Good teachers do not cling to being or nonbeing, having abandoned all kinds of demonic suggestion. When they speak, they do not entangle or bind others. Whatever they say, they do not call it a teacher's explanation; like echoes in a valley, their words fill the land faultlessly. They are worthy of trust and association.

If anyone should say, "I am capable of explaining, I am able to understand; I am the teacher, you are the disciples," this is the same as demonic suggestion and pointless talk. Once you have actually seen the existence of the Way, to say, "This is Buddha, this is not Buddha, this is enlightenment, this is extinction, this is liberation," and so on is to pointlessly express partial knowledge. To lift a finger and say, "This is Zen! This is Tao!" is to utter words that entangle and bind others endlessly. This only increases the ties of seekers. And there are still errors of speech even when they are unspoken.

Be master of mind; don't be mastered by mind. In the incomplete teaching, there is a teacher, there is a guide; in the complete teaching, there is no teacher, and doctrine is not the master. If you are still unable to resort to the mystic mirror, then for the time being resort to the complete teaching, and you will yet have some familiarity with it. As for the incomplete teaching, it is suitable only for unhearing worldlings.

For now, do not depend on anything at all, whether it is there or not; and do not dwell on not depending on anything, and also do not make an understanding of not depending or dwelling, either. This is called great wisdom.

Only a buddha is a great teacher, because there is no second person. The rest are all called outsiders, and what they say is demonic suggestion.

Right now, the point is to explain away dualism. Do not be affected by greed for anything at all, whether it is there or not. As far as untying bonds is concerned, there are no special words or statements to teach people.

If you say there are some particular statements to teach people, or that there is some particular doctrine to give people, this is heresy and demonic suggestion.

You must distinguish complete and incomplete teachings, prohibitive and nonprohibitive words, living and dead words, expressions of healing and sickness, negative and positive metaphors, and generalizing and particularizing expressions.

To say that it is possible to attain buddhahood by cultivation, that there is practice and there is realization, that this mind is enlightened, that the mind itself is Buddha, is Buddha's teaching. This is the incomplete teaching. These are nonprohibitive words, generalizing expressions, words of a one-pound or one-ounce burden. These words are concerned with weeding out impure things. These are words of positive metaphor. These are dead words. These are words for ordinary people.

To say that it is not possible to attain buddhahood by cultivation, that there is no cultivation and no realization, that it is neither mind nor Buddha, is also Buddha's teaching. These are words of the complete teaching, prohibitive words, particularizing words, words of a ten-thousand-pound burden, words of negative metaphor and negative instruction, words concerned with weeding out pure things. These are words for someone of rank in the Way. These are living words.

As long as there are verbal formulations, from entry into the stream all the way up to the tenth stage of enlightenment, everything is in the category of defilement by the dust of doctrine. As long as there are verbal formulations, everything is in the realm of affliction and trouble. As long as there are verbal formulations, everything belongs to the incomplete teaching.

The complete teaching is obedience; the incomplete teaching is transgression. At the stage of buddhahood, there is neither obedience nor transgression; neither the complete nor the incomplete teachings are admitted.

Discern the ground by way of the sprouts; discern the pure by way of the impure. Just be aware, mirrorlike, right now. If you assess mirroring awareness from the standpoint of purity, it is not pure, but absence of mirroring awareness is not pure either, nor is it impure. Nor is it holy or unholy. It is not, furthermore, a matter of seeing the impurity of the water and talking about the problems of impurity in water. If the water were pure, nothing could be said; in fact, speech would defile the water.

If there is a questionless question, there is also speechless explanation. A buddha does not explain truth for the sake of buddhas. In the world of reality where everything is equally suchness, there is no Buddha; no one rescues living beings. A buddha does not remain in buddhahood; this is called the real field of blessings.

You must distinguish host and guest words. If you are affected by greed for anything at all, whether it is there or not, you will be confused and disturbed by everything. Your own mind then becomes the king of demons, and its perceptive functions are in the category of deluding demons.

If your immediate mirroring awareness does not dwell on anything, existent or nonexistent, mundane or transcendent; and yet does not make an understanding of nondwelling and does not even dwell in the absence of understanding, then your own mind is Buddha, and its perceptive functions are in the category of enlightening beings. Master of all mental conditions, its perceptive functions are in the realm of passing phenomena.

It is like waves telling of water; it illumines myriad forms without effort. If you can perceive calmly, you will penetrate the hidden essence and penetrate all time. As it is said, "When psychology has no influence on perception, the ultimate power remains, serving as a guide in all places."

People's natural consciousness is sticky, because they have not trodden the steps to enlightenment. They have stuck fast to various things for a long time. Even as they partake of the hidden essence, they cannot use it as medicine. Even as they hear words beyond conception, they cannot believe completely.

This is why Gautama Buddha spent forty-nine days in silent contemplation under the tree where he was enlightened. Wisdom is obscure, difficult to explain; there is nothing to which it may be likened.

To say people have buddha nature is to slander the buddhas, their Teaching, and their Communities. To say people have no buddha nature is also to slander the buddhas, their Teaching, and their Communities.

To say there is buddha nature is called slander by attachment. To say there is no buddha nature is called slander by falsehood. As it is said, to say buddha nature exists is slander by presumption, and to say it does not exist is slander by repudiation; to say buddha nature both exists and does not exist is slander by contradiction, and to say buddha nature neither exists nor does not exist is slander by meaningless argument.

KUEI-SHAN
Admonitions

As long as you are subject to a life bound by force of habit, you are not free from the burden of the body. The physical being given you by your parents has come into existence through the interdependence of many conditions; while the basic elements thus sustain you, they are always at odds with one another.

Impermanence, aging, and illness do not give people a set time. One may be alive in the morning, then dead at night, changing worlds in an instant. We are like the spring frost, like the morning dew, suddenly gone. How can a tree growing on a cliff or a vine hanging into a well last forever? Time is passing every moment; how can you be complacent and waste it, seeing that the afterlife is but a breath away?

Inwardly strive to develop the capacity of mindfulness; outwardly spread the virtue of uncontentiousness. Shed the world of dust to seek emancipation.

Over the ages you have followed objects, never once turning back to look within. Time slips away; months and years are wasted.

The Buddha first defined precepts to begin to remove the veils of ignorance. With standards and refinements of conduct pure as ice and snow, the precepts rein and concentrate the minds of beginners in respect to what to stop, what to uphold, what to do, and what not to do. Their details reform every kind of crudity and decadence.

How can you understand the supreme vehicle of complete meaning without having paid heed to moral principles? Beware of spending a lifetime in vain; later regrets are useless.

If you have never taken the principles of the teachings to heart, you have no basis for awakening to the hidden path. As you advance in years and grow old, your vanity will not allow you to associate with worthy companions; you know only arrogance and complacency.

Dawdling in the human world eventually produces dullness and coarseness. Unawares, you become weak and senile; encountering events, you face a wall. When younger people ask you questions, you have nothing to say that will guide them. And even if you have something to say, it has nothing to do with the scriptures. Yet when you are treated without respect, you immediately denounce the impoliteness of the younger generation. Angry thoughts flare up, and your words afflict everyone.

One day you will lie in sickness, flat on your back with myriad pains oppressing you. Thinking and pondering from morning to night, your heart will be full of fear and dread. The road ahead is vague, boundless; you do not know where you will go.

Here you will finally know to repent of your errors, but what is the use of trying to dig a well when you're already thirsty? You will regret not having prepared earlier, now that it is late and your faults are so many.

When it is time to go, you shake apart, terrified and trembling. The cage broken, the sparrow flies. Consciousness follows what you have done, like a man burdened with debts, dragged away first by the strongest. The threads of mind, frayed and diffused, tend to fall to whatever is most pressing.

The murderous demon of impermanence does not stop moment to moment. Life cannot be extended; time is unreliable. No one in any realm of being can escape this. Subjection to physical existence has gone on in this way for untold ages.

Our regret is that we were all born in an era of imitation. The age of saints is distant, and Buddhism is decadent. Most people are lazy.

If you pass your whole life half asleep, what can you rely on?

If you only want to sit still with folded hands and do not value even a moment of time, if you do not work diligently at your tasks, then you have no basis for accomplishment. How can you pass a whole life in vain?

When you speak, let it concern the scriptures; in discussion, follow your study of the ancients. Be upright and noble of demeanor, with a lofty and serene spirit.

On a long journey, it is essential to go with good companions; purify your eyes and ears again and again. When you stay somewhere, choose your company; listen to what you have not heard time and again. This is the basis of the saying, "It was my parents who bore me; it was my companions who raised me."

Companionship with the good is like walking through dew and mist; although they do not drench your clothing, in time it becomes imbued with moisture. Familiarity with evil increases false knowledge and views, creating evil day and night. You experience consequences right away, and after death you sink. Once you have lost human life, you will not return ever again, even in ten thousand eons. True words may offend the ear, but do they not impress the heart? If you cleanse the mind and cultivate virtue, conceal your tracks and hide your name, preserve the fundamental and purify the spirit, then the clamor will cease.

If you want to study the Way by intensive meditation and make a sudden leap beyond expedient teachings, let your mind merge with the hidden harbor; investigate its subtleties, determine its most profound depths, and realize its true source.

When you suddenly awaken to the true basis, this is the stairway leading out of materialism. This shatters the twenty-five domains of being in the three realms of existence. Know that everything, inside and outside, is all unreal. Arising from transformations of mind, all things are merely provisional names; don't set your mind on them. As long as feelings do not stick to things, how can things hinder people? Leaving them to the all-pervasive flow of reality, do not cut them off, yet do not continue them either. When you hear sound and see form, all is normal; whether in the relative world or in the transcendental absolute, appropriate function is not lacking.

If there are people of middling ability who are as yet unable to transcend all at once, let them concentrate upon the teaching, closely investigating the scriptures and scrupulously looking into the inner meaning.

Have you not heard it said, "The vine that clings to the pine climbs to the heights; only based on the most excellent foundation may there be widespread weal"? Carefully cultivate frugality and self-control. Do not vainly be remiss, and do not go too far. Then in all worlds and every life there will be sublime cause and effect.

Cease conceptualization; forget about objects; do not be a partner to the dusts. When the mind is empty, objects are quiescent.

Assert mastery; do not follow human sentimentality. The entanglements of the results of actions are impossible to avoid. When the voice is gentle, the echo corresponds; when the figure is upright, the shadow is straight. Cause and effect are perfectly clear; have you no concern?

This illusory body,
this house of dreams:
appearances in emptiness.
There has never been a beginning;
how could an end be determined?
Appearing here, disappearing there,
rising and sinking,
worn and exhausted,
never able to escape the cycle,
when will there ever be rest?
Lusting for the world,
body-mind and the causal nexus
compound the substance of life.
From birth to old age,
nothing is gained;
subjection to delusion comes
from fundamental ignorance.
Take heed that time is passing;
we cannot count on a moment.
If you go through this life in vain,
the coming world will be obstructed.
Going from illusion to illusion
is all due to indulgent senses;
they come and go through mundane routines,
crawling through the triplex world.

Call on enlightened teachers without delay;
approach those of lofty virtue.
Analyze and understand body and mind;
clear away the brambles.
The world is inherently evanescent, empty;
how can conditions oppress you?
Plumb the essence of truth,
with enlightenment as your guide.
Let go of mind and objects both;
do not recall, or recollect.
With the senses free of care,
activity and rest are peaceful, quiet;
with the unified mind unaroused,
myriad things all rest.

KUEI-SHAN
AND YANG-SHAN
Sayings and Dialogues

KUEI-SHAN SAID, "The mind of a Wayfarer is plain and direct, without artificiality. There is no rejection and no attachment, no deceptive wandering mind. At all times seeing and hearing are normal. There are no further details. One does not, furthermore, close the eyes or shut the ears; as long as feelings do not stick to things, that will do.

"Sages since time immemorial have only explained the problems of pollution. If one does not have all that false consciousness, emotional and intellectual opinionatedness, and conceptual habituation, one is clear as autumn water, pure and uncontrived, placid and uninhibited. Such people are called Wayfarers, or free people."

Kuei-shan was asked, "Is there any further cultivation for people who have suddenly awakened?"

Kuei-shan replied, "If they awaken truly, realizing the fundamental, they know instinctively when it happens. The question of cultivation or not is two-sided. Suppose beginners have conditionally attained a moment of sudden awakening to inherent truth, but there are still longstanding habit energies that cannot as yet be cleared all at once. They must be taught to clear away streams of consciousness manifesting habitual activity. That is cultivation, but there cannot be a particular doctrine to have them practice or devote themselves to.

"Having entered into the principle through hearing, as the principle heard is profound and subtle, the mind is naturally completely clear and does not dwell in the realm of confusion. Even if there are hundreds and thousands of subtleties to criticize or commend the times, you must gain stability, gird your loins, and know how to make a living on your own before you can realize them.

"In essence, the noumenal ground of reality does not admit of a single particle, but the methodology of myriad practices does not abandon anything. If you penetrate directly, then the sense of the ordinary and the sacred disappears, concretely revealing the true constant, where principle and fact are not separate. This is the buddhahood of being-as-is."

Kuei-shan asked Yun-yen, "What is the seat of enlightenment?"

Yun-yen said, "Freedom from artificiality."

Yun-yen then asked Kuei-shan the same question. Kuei-shan replied, "The vanity of all things."

Kuei-shan asked Yang-shan, "Of the forty scrolls of the *Nirvana Scripture*, how many are Buddha's talk, and how many are the devil's talk?"

Yang-shan replied, "They're all devil talk."

Kuei-shan said, "Hereafter no one will be able to do anything to you."

Yang-shan asked, "As a temporary event, where do I focus my action?"

Kuei-shan said, "I just want your perception to be correct; I don't tell you how to act."

Kuei-shan passed a water pitcher to Yang-shan. As Yang-shan was about to take it, Kuei-shan withdrew it and said, "What is it?"

Yang-shan responded, "What do *you* see?"

Kuei-shan said, "If you put it that way, why then seek from me?"

Yang-shan said, "That is so, yet as a matter of humanity and righteousness, it is also my own business to pour some water for you."

Kuei-shan then handed Yang-shan the pitcher.

Kuei-shan asked Yang-shan, "How do you understand origin, abiding, change, and extinction?"

Yang-shan said, "At the time of the arising of a thought, I do not see that there is origin, abiding, change, or extinction."

Kuei-shan retorted, "How can you dismiss phenomena?"

Yang-shan rejoined, "What did you just ask about?"

Kuei-shan said, "Origin, abiding, change, and extinction."

Yang-shan concluded, "Then what do you call dismissing phenomena?"

Kuei-shan asked Yang-shan, "How do you understand the immaculate mind?"

Yang-shan replied, "Mountains, rivers, and plains; sun, moon, and stars."

Kuei-shan said, "You only get the phenomena."

Yang-shan rejoined, "What did you just ask about?"

Kuei-shan said, "The immaculate mind."

Yang-shan asked, "Is it appropriate to call it phenomena?"

Kuei-shan said, "You're right."

Yang-shan asked Kuei-shan, "When hundreds and thousands of objects come upon us all at once, then what?"

Kuei-shan replied, "Green is not yellow, long is not short. Everything is in its place. It's none of my business."

A seeker asked Kuei-shan, "What is the Way?"

Kuei-shan replied, "No mind is the Way."

The seeker complained, "I don't understand."

Kuei-shan said, "You should get an understanding of what doesn't understand."

The seeker asked, "What is that which does not understand?"

Kuei-shan said, "It's just you, no one else!" Then he went on to say, "Let people of the present time just realize directly that which does not understand. *This* is your mind; *this* is your Buddha. If you gain some external knowledge or understanding and consider it the Way of Zen, you are out of touch for the time being. This is called hauling waste in, not hauling waste out; it pollutes your mental field. That is why I say it is not the Way."

Yang-shan asked Kuei-shan, "What is the abode of the real Buddha?"

Kuei-shan said, "Using the subtlety of thinking without thought, think back to the infinity of the flames of awareness. When thinking comes to an end, return to the source, where essence and form are eternal and phenomenon and noumenon are nondual. The real Buddha is being-as-is."

Yang-shan said in a lecture, "You should each look into yourself rather than memorize what I say. For beginningless eons you have been turning away from light and plunging into darkness, so illusions are deeply rooted and can hardly be extirpated all at once. That is why we use temporarily set-up, expedient techniques to remove your coarse consciousness. This is like using yellow leaves to stop a child's crying by pretending they are gold; it is not actually true, is it?"

Yang-shan said in a lecture, "If there is a call for it, there is a transaction; no call, no transaction. If I spoke of the source of Zen, I wouldn't find a single associate, let alone a group of five hundred to seven hundred followers. If I talk of one thing and another, then they struggle forward to take it in. It is like fooling children with an empty fist; there's nothing really there.

"I am now talking to you clearly about matters pertaining to sagehood, but do not focus your minds on them. Just turn to the ocean of your own essence and work in accord with reality. You do not need spiritual powers, because these are ramifications of sagehood, and for now you need to know your mind and arrive at its source.

"Just get the root, don't worry about the branches—they'll naturally be there someday. If you haven't gotten the root, you cannot acquire the branches even if you study, using your intellect and emotions. Have you not seen how Master Kuei-shan said, 'When the mentalities of the ordinary mortal and the saint have ended, being reveals true normalcy, where fact and principle are not separate; this is the buddhahood of being-as-is'?"

SUN-CHI

Symbolic Studies

Circles

THE CIRCLE IS a symbol of nirvana as the refuge. It is also
called the sign of the noumenal buddha nature. All people, ordinary folk as well as sages, are related to this: though the sign
does not differ, delusion and understanding are not the same;
that is why there are ordinary mortals and there are sages. In
other words, those who perceive the meaning of the symbol are
called sages, while those who misperceive it are called ordinary
people.

Thus when Nagarjuna was in south India, to expound the
Teaching to a crowd he manifested a transformation of appearance, such that his body looked like the moon hovering over his
chair; only his voice was heard teaching, and his bodily form
was invisible.

A grandee in the crowd by the name of Aryadeva said to the
people, "Do you recognize this sign?"

The people replied, "No. It would take an advanced sage to
understand, wouldn't it?"

Now Aryadeva's mind sense was already quiet, and he in fact
saw the sign, silently sharing in understanding. So he said to

the crowd, "This auspicious sign is the teacher illustrating the buddha nature; it is not the teacher's own body. The image of formless concentration is like the full moon; it means buddha nature."

Before the grandee had even finished speaking, the teacher manifested his own body in the chair and said in verse,

> Physical manifestation of the full moon symbol
> Is used to illustrate the body of buddhas;
> Explaining that the Truth has no such form
> Is to make clear it's not an object of sense.

If someone uses the symbol of the moon orb to pose a question, the word *ox* is written inside the circle to reply.

A circle with an ox inside is the symbol of the ox eating the herb of tolerance. It is also called the symbol of attaining enlightenment by seeing essence.

What is the reasoning? Scripture says, "There is an herb in the Snowy Mountains called Tolerance; a cow that eats it produces ghee." It also says, "If people listen to exposition of great nirvana, then they see the buddha nature." So the herb symbolizes the sublime teaching, the ox symbolizes the potential for sudden enlightenment, and the ghee symbolizes buddhahood. Thus if the ox eats the herb, it produces ghee; if people understand the teaching, they attain correct awakening. Therefore the symbol of the ox eating the herb of tolerance is also called the symbol of perceiving essence and attaining enlightenment.

A circle with three animals beneath it is the symbol of the three vehicles seeking emptiness. Why? When people in the three vehicles hear exposition of true emptiness, they consciously aim for it, not having yet experienced true emptiness. Thus this is represented by three animals below the circle.

If this symbol is used to pose a question, it is answered by attainment of enlightenment through gradual perception of essence.

The circle with an ox inside is the symbol of the white ox on open ground. The open ground stands for the stage of buddhahood; it is also called ultimate emptiness, or emptiness in the absolute sense. The white ox stands for the subtle intelligence of the spiritual body. Thus it is represented by one ox gone into a circle.

Why are three animals placed beneath the moon orb symbol, then answered with one ox inside the moon orb symbol? The three animals below the moon orb symbol represent the three vehicles, while the one ox in the center of the moon orb symbol represents the unitary vehicle. Thus when the temporary vehicles are brought up, the response is manifestation of the reality, leading into experiential realization.

Previously it was said that an ox in the circle is the symbol of an ox eating the herb of tolerance; it was also said that an ox in the circle is a symbol of the white ox on open ground. The symbol is the same, but the explanations are different; yet in spite of the difference in explanations, the circle and the ox are not different. The question then is, if they are not different, why is the symbol expressed twice?

The answer is that even though the circle and ox does not differ, the relative swiftness of perceiving essence differs. That is why the same circle and ox appears in different contexts.

In terms of the difference in swiftness of perceiving essence between the ox that eats the herb of tolerance and the white ox on open ground, which is the slow one and which is the fast one?

The ox eating the herb of tolerance illustrates the sudden perception of reality, as in the *Flower Ornament Scripture*, so it is quick. The white ox on open ground illustrates the ultimate resolution of three vehicles into one. So even though the explanations are not the same, the principle that is realized is not different. So the same symbols are used, to show that principle and knowledge do not differ. It does not mean that the derivations are exactly the same.

A circle with an ox above it is a symbol of cultivating cause in conformity with the result. Why? Even though the initial inspiration may produce correct awakening, nevertheless one's actions and insight are not equal to those of buddhahood. This symbol is to illustrate how application does not go beyond stage; the ancient dictum about "walking in the footsteps of those who arrive at reality" is represented by this symbol.

If this symbol is used to pose a question, the response is a moon disk with a sign of well-being inside. The circle with the sign of well-being inside symbolizes the complete fulfillment of cause and result.

Why is the well-being sign inside the circle a reply to the ox above the circle? Because the ox over the circle symbolizes cultivating cause in accord with result, while the well-being sign inside the circle symbolizes completion of cause and fulfillment of result. When the cause is brought up, the result is illustrated in reply.

A circle with an ox below it symbolizes spiritual practice in quest of emptiness. This is called the reed hut in front of the gate. Enlightening beings seek emptiness, so scripture speaks of "cultivating enlightening practice for three incalculable eons, enduring the unendurable and carrying out the impossible, seeking unremittingly." That is what this symbol illustrates; if it is used to pose a question, the word *king* is written inside a circle in reply.

A circle with a king inside symbolizes gradual witness of reality. Why? If enlightening beings, through eons of practical cultivation, destroy all bedevilments, only then will they attain uncontaminated knowledge of reality and experientially enter the state of buddhahood. Then there are no more habits obstructing them. They are like wise kings who have overcome all rebels, so their countries are peaceful and they have no more enemies interfering with them.

The next two pairs of symbols represent dismissing the unreal to point to the real.

A circle with an ox above and a human inside symbolizes conceptual understanding of the teachings left behind by the Buddha. In other words, if people rely on the universal teaching of the unitary vehicle expounded by Buddha and are well able to analyze and explain it truly, without error, and yet do not realize their own noumenal insight, they are completely dependent on the explanations of another. That is the sense of this symbol.

If this symbol is used to pose a question, it is answered by removing the ox from above the circle, leaving a circle with a human inside.

A circle with a human inside symbolizes perceiving the root and returning to the source. Scripture says, "Return the spirit to abide in the cave of emptiness, overcoming what is difficult to subdue, shedding the bonds of bedevilment; sitting aloof on open ground, the cluster of consciousness is completely nirvanic." That is what this symbolizes.

Why remove the ox above but not the human within the circle? Because the human within the circle represents noumenal insight, while the ox above the circle represents conceptual understanding. Even if people rely on the teachings and analyze the works of the whole Buddhist canon, as long as they have not actualized their own noumenal insight, it is all conceptual understanding. When conceptual interpretation does not arise, then noumenal insight appears, so we erase the ox above the circle and not the human inside it. This is why scripture says, "Just get rid of the sickness, not the prescription."

Why can't ordinary people learn the truth by way of the teachings? If people have wisdom, what do they need with teachings? If they are ordinary people with discriminatory minds, they derive no benefit from depending on doctrines.

Then do the canonical Buddhist teachings have any use? It's not that no one can become enlightened through the teachings, but conceptual interpretation is simply unreal. This is why Buddha chided Ananda, "Even if you memorize the pure principles of the canons of all the buddhas of the ten directions fluently, that will just increase frivolous argumentation." So we should realize that conceptual interpretation of the teachings is of no benefit.

Why do the teachings say, "Those who hear Buddha's teachings all attain sagehood"? It is people of more highly developed faculties who wake right up by way of the teachings, directly actualizing noumenal insight, sure and clear. For those of lesser faculties who do not awaken through the Teaching, conceptual understanding is of no use. But if people of less-developed faculties let the Teaching influence their lives, waiting for another time, who would say there is no benefit? Those who hear the teachings all attain sagehood; the tiniest bit of goodness is a setting forth to arrive at buddhahood—how much more this is so of broad learning in scriptures and treatises!

A circle with a human inside and an ox below symbolizes mistaking your reflection for your head. What is the reasoning? If people do not realize their own inner Buddha and Pure Land but believe in a Buddha and Pure Land in some other realm, they wholeheartedly seek rebirth in the Pure Land to see the Buddha and hear the Teaching. Therefore they diligently practice good deeds and chant the names of the Buddha and the features of the Pure Land. That is what this symbolizes. This is what Master Chih ridiculed when he said, "Those who do not understand that mind itself is Buddha are as if mounted on a donkey looking for a donkey."

If this symbol is used to pose a question, the ox below is removed in reply.

The circle with a human inside symbolizes turning away from your reflection to recognize your head.

Why remove the ox below the circle and not the human inside? When people have not yet awakened true knowledge and have not arrived at true voidness., they focus on seeking a Pure Land and a Buddha in another dimension, so that they might be reborn in the Pure Land, see the Buddha, and hear the Teaching. If people would turn their attention inward, awaken knowledge, and attain true emptiness, then the Buddha and Pure Land within themselves would appear at once, without their having to seek a Pure Land or Buddha outside the mind. So the human inside the circle is not removed, only the ox below the circle.

What is the Buddha within oneself, and the Pure Land within oneself? If people awaken true knowledge and arrive at true emptiness, then true knowledge is Buddha, and emptiness is the Pure Land. If you understand this through experiencing it, where else would you seek a Pure Land and a Buddha? This is why scripture says, "If you're going to keep listening to an external Buddha, why does your inner Buddha not listen to its own listening?"

There are five more symbols, in four pairs.

A semicircle is a symbol of "bringing up a box, seeking a lid," also called the symbol of the half moon awaiting fullness. If this is used to pose a question, another half moon is added in response. Thus the question brings out a box seeking a lid, while the response puts a lid on the box. As the box and cover fit each other, they manifest the sign of the full moon, the circle representing the essence of all buddhas.

An empty circle is a symbol of holding a jade looking for a

match. If this symbol is used to pose a question, a certain word is written inside the circle to reply. Thus the question brings a jade seeking its match, and the one who replies recognizes the gem and acts on that.

A circle with a hook inside symbolizes fishing for continuity. If this is used to pose a question, the character for *human* is added next to the character for *hook*, forming a character *buddha*. Thus the questioner fishes for continuity, and the one who answers follows up to complete a precious vessel.

A circle with *buddha* inside symbolizes having completed the precious vessel. If this is used to pose a question, the character for *land* is written inside the circle to reply.

A circle with *land* inside symbolizes the mystic seal. This is utterly beyond all the preceding symbols and is not contained in the concepts of the teachings.

Three Meanings of Buddhahood
1. Attaining Buddhahood by Realizing Noumenon
2. Attaining Buddhahood by Fulfillment of Application
3. Attaining Buddhahood in Manifestation

Attaining buddhahood by realizing principle, or noumenon, means that with a teacher's instruction you turn your attention around to focus it on the source of your own mind, where there is basically nothing concrete. This is attaining buddhahood without going through a gradual process of myriad practices. This is why scripture says that one attains true enlightenment at the first inspiration, and an ancient said that buddhahood is not far away—just turn your attention around, and there it is.

In the context of attaining buddhahood by realizing noumenon, if you speak of essence there is no thing there at all, but if you talk about the three embodiments, there is a buddha and two bodhisattvas, an enlightened one and two enlightening beings. Although there are three personifications, in the present case of attainment of buddhahood by perceiving essence, the achievement of buddhahood is therefore attributed to Manjushri. That is why the ancients said that Manjushri is the mother of all buddhas, because all buddhas are born from Manjushri, for Manjushri represents true knowledge. All buddhas realize enlightenment by means of true knowledge, so Manjushri is the mother of all buddhas.

As for attaining buddhahood by fulfillment of application, this means that even when you have discovered the true principle of noumenal reality, still you follow the practical commitments of Universal Good, practicing extensive cultivation of the bodhisattva path stage by stage. "Attaining buddhahood by fulfillment of application" refers to comprehensiveness of application and complete fulfillment of knowledge and compassion.

For this reason an ancient said, "The ultimate end of practical application is the original place." So we know that when practical application is complete, it returns to the origin. The origin is the principle, the noumenon.

This principle realized in attainment of buddhahood by fulfillment of practical application is no different from the principle realized in attainment of buddhahood by realization of noumenon. Even though the principle is no different, this latter is called attaining buddhahood by fulfillment of practical application because we arrive at the result by putting the cause into effect.

In referring to attainment of buddhahood by fulfillment of practical application, if we speak in terms of the qualities of fruition, we just speak of attaining buddhahood by the practice of Samantabhadra, or Universal Good. But if we speak in terms of the three embodiments, there is also one buddha with two accompanying bodhisattvas.

Nevertheless, though there are three personifications, now

because we are dealing particularly with attainment of buddha-hood by fulfillment of practice, the merit of attainment of bud-dhahood is in Samantabhadra, so the ancients said that Samantabhadra is the father of the buddhas. When it is said that all buddhas are born of Samantabhadra, this Samantabhadra or Universal Good means myriad practices; all buddhas realize en-lightenment through their myriad practices, so Samantabhadra is the father of all buddhas.

When we speak of one buddha and two bodhisattvas, Vairo-chana Buddha stands for principle, or noumenon, while Man-jushri bodhisattva stands for knowledge, and Samantabhadra bodhisattva stands for practice. Because this principle, knowl-edge, and practice are the same essence, none can be dispensed with.

The one buddha and two bodhisattvas, furthermore, are both central and auxiliary to each other. In terms of the supremacy of the basic essence, Vairochana is central. In terms of the ac-complishment of knowledge seeing essence, Manjushri is cen-tral. In terms of the power of virtue of myriad practices, Samantabhadra is central. Thus Li T'ung-hsuan said, "All bud-dhas attain enlightenment through the great beings Manjushri and Samantabhadra," yet he also said, "Manjushri and Saman-tabhadra are the younger and elder sons of all buddhas." So obviously the three personifications are both central and auxil-iary to one another.

As for attainment of buddhahood in manifestation, after one has realized the principle and one's practice is complete, now that one's own practical attainment of buddhahood is done, one manifests eight aspects of attainment of buddhahood for other people.

The eight aspects of attainment of buddhahood are: descent from the heaven of satisfaction into the womb; dwelling in the womb; emerging from the womb; living in a palace; leaving home; awakening; teaching; and passing away into nirvana. Attainment of buddhahood has eight aspects whereby this is called attainment of buddhahood in manifestation.

It should be realized that the eight aspects of attaining buddhahood are of the embodiments of enjoyment and projection, not of reality. This is why scripture says, "Buddhas do not emerge in the world, nor do they become extinct; it is by the power of their basic commitment that they manifest the state of freedom." This scripture points to the real Buddha within the buddhas of enjoyment and projection. Scripture also says, "It has been infinite eons since I attained buddhahood," indicating that Shakyamuni Buddha had already completed his practice and fully awakened infinite eons earlier and was manifesting the attainment of enlightenment for the sake of other people.

The House of
LIN-CHI

HUANG-PO
Transmission of Mind

THE BUDDHAS AND all living beings are only one mind; there is no other reality. This mind, from beginninglessness, has never been born and never passed away. It is neither blue nor yellow; it has no shape and no form. It does not belong to existence or nonexistence; it does not count as new or old. It is neither long nor short, neither large nor small. It transcends all limiting measurements, all labels, all traces, all oppositions. This very being is it; when you stir thoughts, you turn away from it. It is like space, which has no boundaries and cannot be measured.

This one mind is itself Buddha. Buddha and sentient beings are no different; it's just that sentient beings seek externally, grasping appearances, losing the more they seek. If you try to have Buddha seek Buddha, or use mind to grasp mind, you will never succeed. What you don't realize is that if you stop thoughts and forget ruminations, the Buddha spontaneously appears.

This mind itself is Buddha; buddhas are sentient beings. As sentient beings, this mind is not diminished; as buddhas, this mind is not increased. Even the six perfections, myriad practices, and countless virtues are inherent and do not need to be added by cultivation; when the appropriate circumstances are

43

encountered they are employed, and when those circumstances end they rest.

If you do not believe with certainty that this is Buddha, and want to cultivate practice bound up with forms in order to seek effective application, this is all illusion, contrary to the Way. This mind itself is Buddha; there is no other buddha and no other mind. This mind is clear and pure as space, with no appearance at all; when you arouse the mind and stir thoughts, you turn away from the essence of its reality. This is attachment to appearances; there has never been buddhahood attached to appearances. If you cultivate the myriad practices of six perfections in quest of buddhahood, this is a gradual procedure, but there never has been buddhahood as a gradual procedure. Just realize the one mind, and there is nothing else at all to attain. This is the real Buddha.

Buddhas, sentient beings, and the one mind are no different, like space without adulteration or corruption, like the orb of the sun illumining the four quarters. When the sun rises, its light pervades the land, but space is never bright. When the sun sets, darkness covers the land, but space is never dark. States of light and darkness alternate, but the nature of space remains open and empty, unchanging. So it is also with buddhas, sentient beings, and mind. If you contemplate buddhas as forms of pure illumination and liberation, and you contemplate sentient beings as forms of muddled living and dying in the dark, with this understanding you will never ever attain enlightenment, because you are attached to appearances.

It's just this one mind; there is nothing else at all to attain. Mind itself is Buddha. People who study the Way today do not understand the essence of this mind, so they conceive of another mind on top of this mind, seeking buddhahood externally, cultivating practices attached to appearances. All of this is wrong; it is not the way to enlightenment.

"Respectfully supporting all the buddhas in the universe is not as good as respectfully supporting a single mindless Wayfarer." Why is this so? Mindlessness means total nonsubjectivity, the essence of being-as-is. Inwardly one is immovable as a tree, unstirring as a rock; outwardly one is as free from blockage and resistance as space itself. There is neither subject nor object, no direction or location, no form or appearance, no gain or loss.

People who strive do not dare to enter into this teaching, fearing they will fall into voidness with no place to rest; they withdraw, intimidated. All of them search far and wide for knowledge. That is why those who seek knowledge are numerous as hairs, while those who realize the Way are rare as horns.

Manjushri stands for principle; Samantabhadra stands for practice. The principle here is the principle of true emptiness without resistance; practice here means infinite action detached from appearances. Avalokiteshvara stands for universal compassion; Mahasthamaprapta stands for universal knowledge. Vimalakirti means Pure Name: purity refers to essence; name refers to characteristics; essence and characteristics are not different, hence the title Pure Name. What the various major bodhisattvas represent is all within humanity. It is not apart from one mind; all you have to do is realize it.

People who study the Way today do not value enlightenment within their own minds, so they cling to appearances outside the mind and grasp objects; all of this is contrary to the Way.

As for the "sands of the Ganges River," Buddha explained that the sands do not rejoice when buddhas, bodhisattvas, Indra, Brahma, or any of the gods walk upon them, and the sands are not angered when oxen, goats, bugs, and ants walk on them. The sands have no craving for jewels and perfumes and no aversion to manure and filth. A mind like this is a mindless mind. This is the ultimate; if students of the Way do not plunge right into mindlessness, even if they cultivate practices for eons on end, they will never attain the Way. Captured by the practices of the Three Vehicles, they will be unable to attain liberation.

There are, however, differences in rapidity of realizing this mind. There are those who immediately attain mindlessness on hearing the teaching, and there are those who attain mindlessness only on reaching the Ten Faiths, the Ten Abodes, the Ten Practices, or the Ten Dedications. But whether it takes a long time or a short time, when you attain mindlessness, then you stop; there is nothing more to be cultivated or realized.

Actually, there is nothing attained, but this is actually true, not unreal. The accomplishment of attainment in one instant and attainment at the tenth stage are equal; there is no more deep or shallow.

It's just that when you go through eons you suffer painful toil unreasonably. Evildoing and doing good are both attachment to appearances. If you do evil attached to appearances, you subject yourself to vicious circles unreasonably. If you do good attached to appearances, you suffer the pains of laborious toil unreasonably. None of this is as good as immediately recognizing the basic reality on your own as soon as you hear of it.

This reality is mind; there is no truth outside of mind. This mind itself is truth; there is no mind outside of reality. Mind is inherently mindless; and there is no mindless one, either. If you mindfully try to be mindless, then minding is there.

It's just a matter of silent accord; it is beyond all conception. That is why it is said that there is no way to talk about it, no way to think about it.

This mind is pure at the source. Buddhas and ordinary human beings both have it. All living beings are one and the same body with all buddhas and bodhisattvas; it is only because of differences in their subjective thoughts that they create all sorts of activities, with their various results.

Basically there is nothing concrete in buddhahood; it is just

open perception, serene clarity, and subtle bliss. When you realize it profoundly in yourself, this is directly it—complete fulfillment, with no further lack. Even if you exert yourself at
spiritual exercises for three incalculable eons, going through all
the stages and grades, when you reach that one instant of realization, you have just realized the Buddha within yourself; you
have not added anything at all. Rather, you will see your eons
of effort as the confused behavior of dreams.

This is why the Tathagata said, "In supreme perfect enlightenment I have not acquired anything. If I had acquired anything, Dipankara Buddha would not have given me direction."
He also said, "This truth is impartial, without high or low; this
is called enlightenment." This is the mind pure at the source,
impartial in respect to sentient beings, buddhas, worlds, mountains and rivers, forms, formlessness, everything through the
universe, with no image of other or self.

This mind pure at the source is intrinsically always completely clear and fully aware, but worldly people do not realize
it; they only recognize perception and cognition as mind, so they
are shrouded by perception and cognition. That is why they do
not see the very essence of their spiritual luminosity. If they
would just directly be mindless, that very essence would appear
of itself, like the sun rising into the sky, lighting up everywhere,
with no further obstruction.

So students of the Way, only recognizing the actions and
movements of perception and cognition, empty out their perception and cognition, so their minds have no road to go on,
and they attain no penetration. Just recognize the basic mind in
perception and cognition, realizing all the while that the basic
mind does not belong to perception and cognition and yet is not
apart from perception and cognition.

Just do not conceive opinions and interpretations on top of
perception and cognition, and do not stir thoughts on percep-

tion and cognition. Do not seek mind apart from perception and cognition, either, and do not try to get to reality by rejecting perception and cognition. When you are neither immersed nor removed, neither dwelling nor clinging, free and independent, then nothing is not a site of enlightenment.

Worldly people who hear it said that the buddhas all communicate the truth of mind think it means there is some special truth in the mind to realize or grasp, so they wind up using mind to search for mind. They do not realize that mind itself is the truth, and the truth itself is mind. It will not do to use mind to seek mind, for that way you will never realize it, even in a million years. It is better to be mindless right away, and then you find fundamental reality.

It is like the story of the wrestler who was unaware that a gem had been embedded in his forehead, and he looked elsewhere for it. He went all over the place but ultimately couldn't find it, until someone who knew pointed it out to him, whereupon he himself saw the original gem as it had been all along.

So it is that people who study the Way stray from their own original mind, not recognizing it as Buddha, and wind up seeking outwardly, undertaking practices and exercises, depending on a process for realization. Even though they seek diligently for eons, they never attain the Way. It is better to be mindless right away, realizing for certain that all things are originally without existence, ungraspable, based on nothing; they abide nowhere and are neither subjective nor objective. If you do not stir errant thoughts, you will immediately realize enlightenment.

LIN-CHI

Sayings

PEOPLE WHO STUDY Buddhism in the present day should for now seek truly accurate vision and understanding. Then life and death will not influence you, and you will be free to leave or to stay. You do not need to seek the extraordinary, for the extraordinary will come of itself.

The worthies of old all had means of emancipating people. What I teach people just requires you not to take on the confusions of others. If you need to act, then act, without any further hesitation or doubt.

When students today do not realize this, where is the problem? The problem is in not spontaneously trusting. If you do not trust yourself completely, you will then hurriedly go along with whatever happens in all situations; as you are caused to undergo changes by those myriad situations, you cannot be independent.

If you were able to put a stop to the mentality in which every thought is running after something, then you would be no different from a Zen master or a buddha. Do you want to know what a Zen master or a buddha is? Simply that which is immediately present, listening to the Teaching. It is just because students do not trust completely that they seek outwardly. Even if they get something by seeking, it is all literary excellence; they never attain the living meaning of the masters.

Make no mistake about it; if you do not find it now, you will repeat the same routines for myriad eons, a thousand times over again, following and picking up on objects that attract you, born in the bellies of donkeys and oxen.

According to my view, we are no different from Shakyamuni Buddha. Today, in your various activities, what do you lack? The spiritual light coursing through your six senses has never been interrupted. If you can see in this way, you will simply be free of burdens all your life.

The world is unstable, like a house on fire. This is not a place where you stay long. The murderous haunt of impermanence comes upon you in a flash, no matter whether you are rich or poor, old or young. If you want to be no different from a Zen master or a buddha, just do not seek outwardly.

The pure light of your mind in a single moment of thought is the reality-body Buddha in your own house. The nondiscriminatory light of your mind in a single moment of thought is the reward-body Buddha in your own house. The nondifferentiated light of your mind in a single moment of thought is the projection-body Buddha in your own house. These three kinds of embodiment are none other than the person who is listening to the teaching right here and now, but it is only by not seeking outwardly that one has these effective functions.

According to professors of scriptures and treatises, the three embodiments are the ultimate model, but in my view this is not so. These three embodiments are names, words; they are also three kinds of dependence. An ancient said, "Embodiments are established based on meaning; the lands are discussed based on substance." The embodiment of the nature of reality and the land of the nature of reality are obviously reflections of a light; now you should get to know the person who is manipulating the reflections of the light—this is the root source of the buddhas. Everywhere is your way home.

The fact is that your physical body cannot expound the Teaching or listen to the Teaching. Your lungs, stomach, liver, and gallbladder cannot expound the Teaching or listen to the Teaching. Space cannot expound the Teaching or listen to the Teaching. So what can expound the Teaching and listen to the Teaching? It is the immediately present, clearly obvious, completely formless solitary light; this is what can expound the Teaching and listen to the Teaching. If you can see in this way, you will be no different from a Zen master or a buddha.

Just do not allow any more interruptions at any time, and everything that you see is It. Just because feelings arise, knowledge is blocked; changes in conceptions result in changes in actualities. That is why you keep repeating the same routines in the world and suffer a variety of miseries.

In my view, nothing is not extremely profound; nothing is not liberated. The reality of mind has no form but pervades the ten directions. In the eyes it is called seeing, in the ears it is called hearing, in the nose it smells, in the mouth it speaks, in the hands it grips, and in the feet it steps. Basically it is a single spiritual light, differentiated into a sixfold combination. Once the whole mind is as nothing, you are liberated wherever you are.

What do I mean when I say this? It is just because you are unable to stop the whole mentality of seeking that you get hooked on useless actions and states of other people who lived a long time ago. If you take my view, you will sit at the head of the psychic and physical embodiments of Buddha: those at the tenth stage, with fulfilled hearts, will be like migrant laborers; those who have attained equivalent and ineffable enlightenment will be like people in fetters and chains; saints and self-illuminates will be like privy ordure; enlightenment and nirvana will be like donkey-tethering stakes.

Why so? You have these obstacles only because you have not realized the emptiness of the eons. Genuine Wayfarers are never like this; they just dissolve their history according to conditions, dressing according to circumstances, acting when they need to act, and sitting when they need to sit, without any idea of seeking the fruits of buddhahood.

Why are they like this? An ancient said, "If you are going to contrive activities to seek buddhahood, then buddhahood is a major sign of birth and death."

Time is to be valued! You just try to learn Zen or Tao on the surface as something outside yourself, learning to recognize terms and slogans, seeking "buddhahood," seeking "mastery," seeking "teachers," considering them conceptually. Make no mistake about it—you have but one father and mother, so what more are you seeking? Turn your attention back upon yourself and observe.

An ancient said "Yajnadatta lost his head, but when his searching stopped, then he had no troubles." What you should do is be normal; don't act imitatively.

There is a kind of shaveling who does not know good from bad, who sees spirits and ghosts, points out this and pictures that, and makes a fuss about sun and rain. All who are like this will have to pay back their debts, someday swallowing hot iron pills in front of the king of the underworld. Once men and women of good families get charmed by this kind of fox, they hoke up wonders, blind to the fact that one day they will be charged for their meals.

It is absolutely necessary for you to seek to obtain genuinely accurate insight and understanding. Then you can travel freely anywhere and avoid being confused by the common sort of spiritual charmer.

It is the one without obsession who is noble. Just do not act in a contrived manner; simply be normal. When you go searching elsewhere outside yourself, your whole approach is already mistaken. You just try to seek buddhahood, but buddhahood is just a name, an expression—do you know the one who is doing the searching?

The buddhas and Zen masters of all times and places have emerged only on account of search for truth. Present-day seekers are also in search of truth. Only when you attain truth will you be done; until you have attained it, you will repeat your former ways.

What is the truth? The truth is the reality of mind. The reality of mind is formless and pervades the ten directions. It is being used presently, right before your eyes, yet people do not trust it sufficiently, so they accept terms and expressions, seeking to assess Buddhism conceptually in the written word. They are as far away as the sky is from earth.

What truth am I talking about? I am talking about the truth of the ground of mind, which can enter into the ordinary and the sacred, into the pure and the polluted, into the absolute and the conventional, and yet is not absolute or conventional, ordinary or sacred, but is able to give names to all the absolute, conventional, ordinary, and sacred. Someone who has realized this cannot be labeled by the absolute or the conventional, by the ordinary or the sacred. If you can grasp it, then use it, without labeling it any more. This is called the mystic teaching.

My teaching is different from that of everyone else. Even if Manjushri and Samantabhadra were to appear before me, each manifesting an embodiment to ask about the teaching, as soon as they addressed me I would already have distinguished them. As I sit in peace, if any more followers of the Way come to see me, I discern them all completely. Why is it like this? Because my view is distinct: externally I do not grasp the ordinary or the sacred; internally I do not dwell on the fundamental; seeing all the way through, I no longer doubt or err.

There is no place for exertion of effort in Buddhism; it is just a matter of being normal and unobsessed, taking care of bodily functions, dressing and eating, lying down when tired. Fools laugh at me; it is the wise who understand this. An ancient said, "Those who work on externals are all ignoramuses."

For now, be the master wherever you are, and then wherever you stand is reality, and situations that come up cannot move you. Even if you have existing habit energy that would impel you to evil deeds, it naturally becomes an ocean of liberation.

Students today do not know the truth at all. They are like goats nosing around, taking whatever they find into their mouths. They cannot distinguish the servant from the master, the guest from the host. People like this enter the path with the wrong attitude; they cannot enter into clamorous situations, yet they call themselves genuine renunciants. In fact they are really worldlings.

As for renunciants, they must master constant truth and authenticity of insight and understanding. They must distinguish Buddha from the devil, they must distinguish the real from the false, and they must distinguish the ordinary from the holy. If they can make these distinctions, they can be called true renunciants.

Those who cannot distinguish devil from Buddha are actually leaving one house to enter another. They may be said to be creating karma; they cannot be called real renunciants. Now there is a confusion of Buddha and devil, like water and milk mixed together. They can only be separated by an expert.

As for Wayfarers with enlightened eyes, they strike down both devil and Buddha. If you love the holy and despise the ordinary, you are bobbing in the ocean of birth and death.

What are the Buddha and the devil?

A moment of doubt in the mind is a devil. If you realize all things are unborn, and mind is like an illusory projection, so that there is no longer a single particle, a single phenomenon, but everywhere is immaculate purity, this is Buddha.

However, Buddha and devil represent the two realms of purity and defilement; in my own view, there is neither Buddha nor mortal being, there is neither antiquity nor present; those who get it do so at once, without taking a certain time. There is no cultivation, no realization, no gain, no loss. At all times there is nothing else. Even if there were something beyond this, I would say it is like a dream, like a projection. This is what I always say.

The immediate solitary light clearly listening is unobstructed everywhere, pervading the ten directions, free in the three realms, entering into the differentiations in objects without being changed. In an instant it enters the cosmos of realities: meeting buddhas, it talks about buddhas; meeting Zen masters, it talks about Zen masters; meeting saints, it talks about saints; meeting ghosts, it talks about ghosts. Within a single thought, it roams in lands everywhere teaching people; its omnipresent pure radiance pervades the ten directions.

Now you know there is basically nothing to be obsessed with. It's just because you do not trust completely that your thoughts run in search. Ignoring your own head, you look for another head, unable to stop yourself.

Bodhisattvas of the complete all-at-once path manifest their bodies in the cosmos of realities, disdaining the ordinary and seeking the holy within pure lands. Types like this have not yet forgotten grasping and rejection; mindfulness of pollution and purity is still there. The view of the Zen school is not like this; it is right now, no other time.

What I say is all temporary medicine for curing illness; there is no real doctrine at all. If you can see in this way, you are a true renunciant; you can use a thousand ounces of gold a day.

Do not hastily let teachers give you a stamp of approval, claiming, "I understand Zen, I understand Tao." They may talk glibly, but they are making hellish karma.

Genuine students of the Way do not look for the faults of the world; what is most urgent is to seek real true insight and understanding. If you attain real true insight, it must be complete and clear before you are finished.

YUAN-WU
Essentials of Mind

WHEN THE FOUNDER of Zen came to China from India, he did not set up written or spoken formulations; he only pointed directly to the human mind. Direct pointing just refers to what is inherent in everyone: the whole being appearing responsively from within the shell of ignorance, it is not different from the sages of time immemorial. That is what we call the natural, real, inherent nature, fundamentally pure, luminous and sublime, swallowing and spitting out all of space, the single solid realm alone and free of the senses and objects.

With great capacity and great wisdom, just detach from thought and cut off sentiments, utterly transcending ordinary conventions. Using your own inherent power, take it up directly right where you are, like letting go your hold over a mile-high cliff, freeing yourself and not relying on anything anymore, causing all obstruction by views and understanding to be thoroughly removed, so that you are like a dead man without breath, and reach the original ground, attaining great cessation and great rest, which the senses fundamentally do not know and which consciousness, perception, feelings, and thoughts do not reach.

After that, in the cold ashes of a dead fire, it is clear everywhere; among the stumps of dead trees everything illumines: then you merge with solitary transcendence, unapproachably high. Then there is no more need to seek mind or seek Buddha: you meet them everywhere and find they are not obtained from outside.

The hundred aspects and thousand facets of perennial enlightenment are all just this: it is mind, so there is no need to still seek mind; it is Buddha, so why trouble to seek Buddha anymore? If you make slogans of words and produce interpretations on top of objects, then you will fall into a bag of antiques and after all never find what you are looking for.

This is the realm of true reality where you forget what is on your mind and stop looking. In a wild field, not choosing, picking up whatever comes to hand, the obvious meaning of Zen is clear in the hundred grasses. Indeed, the green bamboo, the clusters of yellow flowers, fences, walls, tiles, and pebbles use the teaching of the inanimate; rivers, birds, trees, and groves expound suffering, emptiness, and selflessness. This is based on the one true reality, producing unconditional compassion, manifesting uncontrived, supremely wondrous power in the great jewel light of nirvana.

An ancient master said, "Meeting a companion on the Way, spending a life together, the whole task of study is done." Another master said, "If I pick up a single leaf and go into the city, I move the whole of the mountain." That is why one ancient adept was enlightened on hearing the sound of pebbles striking bamboo, while another was awakened on seeing peach trees in bloom. One Zen master attained enlightenment on seeing the flagpole of a teaching center from the other side of a river. Another spoke of the staff of the spirit. One adept illustrated Zen realization by planting a hoe in the ground; another master spoke of Zen in terms of sowing the fields. All of these instances were bringing out this indestructible true being, allowing people to visit a greatly liberated true teacher without moving a step.

Carrying out the unspoken teaching, attaining unhindered eloquence, thus they forever studied all over from all things, embracing the all-inclusive universe, detaching from both abstract and concrete definitions of buddhahood, and transcendentally realizing universal, all-pervasive Zen in the midst of all activities. Why necessarily consider holy places, teachers' abodes, or religious organizations and forms prerequisite to personal familiarity and attainment of realization?

Once a seeker asked a great Zen teacher, "I, so-and-so, ask: what is the truth of Buddhism?" The teacher said, "You are so-and-so." At that moment the seeker was enlightened. As it is said, "What comes from you returns to you."

An ancient worthy, working in the fields in his youth, was breaking up clumps of earth when he saw a big clod, which he playfully smashed with a fierce blow. As it shattered, he was suddenly greatly enlightened.

After this he acted freely, becoming an unfathomable person, often manifesting wonders. An old master brought this up and said, "Mountains and rivers, indeed the whole earth was shattered by this man's blow. Making offerings to the buddhas does not require a lot of incense." How true these words are!

The ultimate Way is simple and easy, yet profoundly deep. From the beginning it does not set up steps—standing like a wall a mile high is called the basic fodder. Therefore ancient buddhas have been known to carry out this teaching by silence.

Still there are adepts who wouldn't let them go at that, much less if they got into the marvelous and searched for the mysterious, spoke of mind and discoursed on nature, having sweaty shirts sticking to their flesh, unable to remove them—that would just seem all the more decrepit.

The example of the early Zen founders was exceptionally outstanding. The practical strategies of the classical masters were immediately liberating. Like dragons racing, tigers running, like the earth turning and the heavens revolving, in all circumstances they vivified people, ultimately without trailing mud and water.

As soon as they penetrated the ultimate point in truth, those since time immemorial who have realized great enlightenment have been fast as falcons, swift as hawks, riding the wind, dazzling in the sun, their backs brushing the blue sky.

Penetrate directly through to freedom and make it so that there is not the slightest obstruction at any time, twenty-four hours a day, with the realization pervading in all directions, rolling up and rolling out, capturing and releasing, not occupying even the rank of sage, much less being in the ordinary current.

Then your heart will be clear, comprehending the present and the past. Picking up a blade of grass, you can use it for the body of Buddha; taking the body of Buddha, you can use it as a blade of grass. From the first there is no superiority or inferiority, no grasping or rejection.

It is simply a matter of being alive to meet the situation: sometimes you take away the person but not the world; sometimes you take away the world but not the person; and sometimes both are taken away; and sometimes neither is taken away.

Transcending convention and sect, completely clear and free, how could you just want to trap people, to pull the wool over their eyes, to turn them around, to derail them? It is necessary to get to the reality and show them the fundamental thing in each of them, which is independent and uncontrived, which has nothing to it at all, and which is great liberation.

This is why the ancients, while in the midst of activity in the world, would first illuminate it, and as soon as there was the slightest obstruction, they would cut it off entirely. Even so they could hardly find anyone who could manage to learn this—how could they compare to these people who drag each other through the weeds, draw each other into assessments and judgments of words and deeds, make nests, and bury the sons and daughters of others?

Clearly we know that these latter people are "wetting the bed with their eyes open," while those other, clear-eyed people would never make such slogans and conventions. With a robust and powerful spirit that astounds everyone, you should aim to truly inherit this school of Zen: with every exclamation, every stroke, every act, every objective, you face reality absolutely and annihilate all falsehood. As it is said, "Once the sharp sword has been used, you should hone it right away."

When your insight penetrates freely and its application is clear, then when going into action in the midst of all kinds of complexity and complication, you yourself can turn freely without sticking or lingering and without setting up any views or maintaining any state, flowing freely: "When the wind blows, the grasses bend."

When you enter enlightenment in actual practice, you penetrate to the profound source, cultivating this until you realize freedom of mind, harboring nothing in your heart. Here even understanding cannot attain it, much less not understanding.

Just be this way twenty-four hours a day, unfettered, free from bondage. From the first do not keep thoughts of subject and object, of self and senses, or even of Buddhism. This is the realm of no mind, no fabrication, no object—how could it be fathomed or measured by worldly brilliance, knowledge, intelligence, or learning, without the fundamental basis?

Did the Zen founder actually "bring" this teaching when he

came to China from India? He just pointed directly to the inherent nature in every one of us, to let us get out completely, clear and clean, and not be stained by so much false knowledge and false consciousness, delusory conceptions, and judgments.

Study must be true study. A true teacher does not lead you into a nest of weeds but cuts directly through so that you meet with realization, shedding the sweaty shirt sticking to your skin, making the heart empty and open, without the slightest sense of the ordinary or the holy. Since you do not seek outside, real truth is there, resting peacefully, immutable. No one can push you away, even a thousand sages—having attained a pure, clean, and naked state, you pass through the other side of the empty eon, and even the prehistoric buddhas are your descendants. Why even speak of seeking from others?

The Zen masters were all like this, ever since the founders. Take the example of the Sixth Grand Master: he was an illiterate woodcutter in south China, but when he came and met the Fifth Grand Master, at their first meeting he opened his heart and clearly passed through to freedom.

So even though the saints and sages are mixed in with others, one should employ appropriate means to clearly point out what is inherent in everyone, regardless of their level of intelligence.

Once you merge your tracks in the stream of Zen, spend the days silencing your mind and studying with your whole being, knowing this great cause is not gotten from anyone else. It is just a matter of bearing up bravely and strongly, ever progressing, day by day shedding, day by day improving, like pure gold smelted and refined hundreds and thousands of times.

As it is essential to getting out of the dusts and it is basic to helping people, it is most necessary to be thoroughly penetrating and free in all ways, reaching to peace without doubt and realizing great potential and great action.

This work lies in one's inner conduct: in everyday life's varied mix of myriad circumstances, in the dusty hubbub, amidst the ups and downs and conditions, appear and disappear without being turned around by any of it. Instead, you can actively turn it around. Full of life, immune to outside influences, this is your own measure of power.

On reaching empty, frozen silence, there is no duality between noise and quiet. Even when it comes to extraordinary words, marvelous statements, unique acts, and absolute perspectives, you just level them with one measure. Ultimately they have no right or wrong, it's all in how you use them.

When you have continued grinding and polishing yourself like this for a long time, you will be free in the midst of birth and death and look upon society's useless honor and ruinous profit as like dust in the wind, phantoms in dreams, flowers in the sky. Passing unattached through the world, would you not then be a great saint who has left the dusts?

Whenever the Zen master known as the Bone Breaker was asked a question, he would just answer, "Bone's broken." This is like an iron pill, undeniably strict. If you can fully comprehend it, you will be a true lion of the Zen school.

Once a great National Teacher of Zen asked another Zen master, "How do you see all extraordinary words and marvelous expressions?" The Zen master said, "I have no fondness for them." The National Teacher said, "This is your own business."

When Zen study reaches this point, one is pure, clean, and dry, not susceptible to human deceptions.

The House of
TS'AO-TUNG

Yao-shan

Master guides only teach preservation; if greed or anger arises, you must ward it off, not letting it touch you. If you want to know how to do this, then you must bear up like a dead tree or a rock.

There are really no ramifications to be attained, but even so, you should still see for yourself. It will not do to deny verbal expression entirely. I am now speaking to you in order to reveal that which has no speech; that originally has no features like ears or eyes.

Someone asked, "How is it that there are six courses of mundane existence?"

Yao-shan said, "Although I am within this circle, I am basically not affected."

Someone asked, "How is it when one does not comprehend the afflictions within one's being?"

Yao-shan said, "What are the afflictions like? I want you to think about it. There is even a type who just memorizes words

on paper; most of them are confused by the scriptures and treatises. I have never read the scriptures or treatises. You have
fluctuating minds simply because you are confused by things
and go through changes, at a loss, inwardly unstable. Even before you have learned a single saying, half an expression, a
scripture, or a treatise, already you talk this way about 'enlightenment,' 'nirvana,' the mundane and the transmundane; if you
understand in this way, then this is birth and death. If you are
not bound by this gain and loss, then there is no birth and death.
You see teachers of discipline talking about stuff like 'naihsar-
gika' and 'dukkata'—this above all is the root of birth and death!

"Even so, when you examine birth and death thoroughly, it
cannot be grasped. From the buddhas above to insects below, all
have these differences of long and short, good and bad, big and
small. If it doesn't come from outside, where is there some idler
digging hells to await you?

"Do you want to know the path of hell? It is boiling and
broiling right now. Do you want to know the path of hungry
ghosts? It is presently being more false than true, so people
cannot trust you. Do you want to know the path of animality?
It is presently disregarding humanity and justice and not distinguishing friend from stranger—do you need to wear fur and
horns, to be butchered and hung upside down? Do you want to
know humans and angels? It is present pure conduct. To guarantee that you will escape falling into the other states, above all
do not abandon this.

"This is not easily attained. You must stand atop the summit
of the highest mountain and walk on the bottom of the deepest
ocean. It is not easy to apply this, but only when you have done
so will you have a little realization.

"All who come forward today are people of many obsessions;
I am looking for a simpleton, but cannot find one. Don't just
memorize sayings in books and consider that to be your own

vision and knowledge, looking down on others who do not understand. People like this are all incorrigible heretics. This
mentality simply does not hit the mark; you must examine carefully and understand thoroughly.

"This kind of talk is still within the bounds of the world.
Don't waste your lives. At this point there is even more subtlety
and detail; don't consider it idle, for you should know it. Take
care."

Yun-yen
Sayings

One day Yun-yen said to a group, "There is an offspring of someone's house who can answer any question."

Tung-shan asked, "How many books does he have in his house?"

Yun-yen said, "There is not even a single letter."

Tung-shan asked, "Then how did he get so much knowledge?"

Yun-yen said, "Never sleeping, day or night."

As Yun-yen was sweeping the grounds, Kuei-shan said, "Too busy!"

Yun-yen said, "You should know there is one who is not busy."

Kuei-shan said, "Then there is a second moon."

Yun-yen stood the broom up and said, "Which moon is this?"

Kuei-shan lowered his head and left. Hsuan-sha heard about this and said, "Precisely the second moon!"

As Yun-yen was making straw sandals, Tung-shan said to him, "If I ask you for perception, can I get it?"

Yun-yen replied, "To whom did you give away yours?"

Tung-shan said, "I have none."

Yun-yen said, "If you had, where would you put it?"

Tung-shan said nothing.

Yun-yen asked, "What about that which asks for perception; is that perception?"

Tung-shan said, "It is not perception."

Yun-yen disapproved.

Yun-yen asked a nun, "Is your father still alive?"

She said, "Yes."

Yun-yen asked, "How old is he?"

She said, "Eighty years old."

Yun-yen said, "You have a father who is not eighty years old; do you know?"

She replied, "Is this not 'the one who comes thus'?"

Yun-yen said, "That is just a descendant!"

A monk asked, "How is it when one falls into the realm of demons the moment a thought occurs?"

Yun-yen said, "Why did you come from the realm of buddhas?"

The monk had no reply.

Yun-yen said, "Understand?"

The monk said, "No."

Yun-yen said, "Don't say you don't comprehend; even if you do comprehend, you're just beating around the bush."

TUNG-SHAN

Song of Focusing the Precious Mirror

THE TEACHING of Being-As-Is
Has been intimated by the enlightened;
Now that you have gotten it,
You should keep it well.

A silver bowl full of snow
And a heron hidden in moonlight
Are similar but not the same;
Put them together, and they're distinct.

The meaning is not in words,
Yet responds to emerging potential.
There's a tendency to create clichés,
Slipping into retrospection, at a standstill.

Rejection and attachment are both wrong;
It is like a ball of fire.
Even to put it in literary form
Subjects it to defilement.

In the middle of night is just when it's bright;
At dawn it does not appear.

Acting as a guide for people,
Its function removes miseries.

Although it is not contrived,
It is not without speech.

It is like looking into a precious mirror,
Form and reflection beholding each other:
You are not it;
It is you.

It is like a baby,
With all its faculties,
Neither going nor coming,
Neither rising nor standing,
Babbling and babbling,
Speaking without saying anything,
Never getting concrete
Because its speech is not correct.

In the six lines of the Fire hexagram,
Relative and absolute integrate;
Stacked up, they make three;
Completion of the transformation makes five.
It is like the taste of a five-flavored herb,
Like the thunderbolt implement.

The subtle is contained within the absolute;
Inquiry and response arise together,
Conveying the source as well as the process,
Including integration as well as the way.

Merging is auspicious;
Do not violate it.

Naturally real, yet subtle,
It is not in confusion or enlightenment.

Under the right conditions, at the right time,
It shines bright in serene tranquillity.
It is so minute it fits where there's no room;
It is so immense it is beyond direction and location.
The slightest deviation
Means failure of attunement.

Now there are sudden and gradual,
On which are set up approaches to the source.
Once approaches to the source are distinguished,
Then there are guidelines and rules.
When the source is reached, the approach thus finished,
True eternity still flows.

To be outwardly still while inwardly stirring
Is to be like a tethered colt, a trapped rat.
Sages of yore took pity on this
And gave out teachings for it.

The way confusion goes,
Even black's considered white;
When confused imagination ends,
Mind in its simplicity realizes itself.

If you want to conform to the perennial way,
Please observe ancient precedent:
When about to fulfill buddhahood,
One meditated under a tree for ten eons,
Like a tiger wounded, like a horse tied.

Because of the existence of the lowly,
There are precious furnishings and fine clothes;

Because of the existence of the unusual,
There are house cats and cattle.

With skill an archer can hit a target
A hundred paces away,
But the meeting of arrow points
Has nothing to do with skill.

When a wooden man begins to sing,
A stone woman gets up to dance.
This cannot be reached by subjective perception;
How could it be thought about?

A minister serves the ruler,
A son obeys his father:
Not to obey is disobedience,
Not to serve is not helping.

Practice unknown, work in secret,
Being like one who is ignorant.
If you can achieve continuity,
This is called mastery of mastery.

Secret of the Mind Elixir

I have a medicine called elixir of mind;
For years it's been refined in the oven of afflictions,
Till I recognized its unchanging color in the matrix
Shining with radiance illuminating the universe.

It opens the eye of reality to see with minute precision;
It can change the ordinary mortal into a sage instantly.

To discern the real and the false to complete the work,
See to refinement at all times.

It has no shape or form; it is not square or round.
There are no things in words; there are no words in things.
Deliberate exploitation is contrary to true function;
When meditating with no intention, everything is Zen.

It neither goes dead nor gets aroused;
Everything is at its command.
Even the land, wherever the place,
When put in this oven is It.

My idea is to have no particular idea;
My knowledge is to have no particular knowledge.
There is no uniformity, no indifference;
When the appearance does not change, it's harder to discern.
When nothing more appears within,
Don't use anything to stabilize it;
Experiential merging with real emptiness
Is not cultivation.

Dialogues of Tung-shan

Tung-shan asked a monk, "Where have you come from?"
  The monk replied, "From a journey to a mountain."
  Tung-shan asked, "And did you reach the peak?"
  The monk said, "Yes."
  Tung-shan asked, "Was there anyone on the peak?"
  The monk answered, "No."
  Tung-shan said, "Then you didn't reach the peak."
  The monk retorted, "If I didn't reach the peak, how could I
know there was no one there?"
  Tung-shan said, "I had doubted this fellow."

As Tung-shan was eating some fruit with Tai, leader of the assembly, he posed this question: "There is one thing supporting heaven and earth; absolutely black, it is always in the midst of activity, yet activity cannot contain it. Where is the fault?"

Tai answered, "The fault is in the activity."

Tung-shan had the fruit tray removed.

Yun-chu built a hut on the mountain peak and didn't come down to the communal hall for days. Tung-shan asked him, "Why haven't you been coming for meals recently?"

Yun-chu said, "An angel comes every day bringing me an offering."

Tung-shan said, "I thought you were an enlightened man, but you still have such a view. Come see me this evening."

That evening Yun-chu went to Tung-shan, who called him by name. When Yun-chu responded, Tung-shan said, "Don't think good, don't think bad—what is this?"

Yun-chu returned to his hut and sat in complete silence and stillness, so the angel couldn't find him. After three days like this, the angel disappeared.

When Ts'ao-shan left Tung-shan, Tung-shan asked him, "Where are you going?"

Ts'ao-shan said, "To an unchanging place."

Tung-shan retorted, "If it is an unchanging place, how can there be any going?"

Ts'ao shan replied, "The going is also unchanging."

Tung-shan's Self-Admonition

Don't seek fame or fortune, glory or prosperity. Just pass this life as is, according to circumstances. When the breath is gone, who is in charge? After the death of the body, there is only an empty name.

When your clothes are worn, repair them over and over; when you have no food, work to provide. How long can a phantomlike body last? Would you increase your ignorance for the sake of its idle concerns?

Tung-shan's Five Ranks: Ts'ao-shan's Elucidation

The absolute state is relative; when it is discerned in the relative, this is fulfillment of both meanings.

The fact that the absolute state is relative is because it is not the opposite of any thing. But even though it is not the opposite of any thing, nevertheless it is there.

When there is no function in the absolute, then it is relative; total function is completeness. This is "both meanings."

What is "total"? One who does not look back is one who has attained. The absolute state does not come from illumination: it is so whether or not a buddha emerges in the world. That is why all sages resort to the absolute state to attain realization.

The relative within the absolute is inherent in this state; above all, don't cause disturbance.

When students choose solitary liberation outside things and stand up before the sages and declare that this is the absolute state, ultimately complete, in reality they are limiting the absolute state. Sayings like this are what the ancients referred to as the traces of passing still remaining. They have not yet attained the unspoken within the spoken. It is said, furthermore, that this is not the absolute state, because there is something said in the words. This could be called defective integration; it cannot be called mutual integration.

The relative state, though relative, still fulfills both meanings; discerned within conditions, this is the unspoken within the spoken.

This is because no aim is defined in function; when no aim is defined, that means it is really not fixed function.

The relative state, though relative, still fulfills both meanings in that there is no thing and no attachment in the function; this is both meanings. Although it is clarified in function, because it is not done violence in speech, here one can speak all day and yet it is as if one had not spoken.

The relative state is actually complete; this also involves being unattached in the midst of conditions.

There may be emergence in the absolute; this is the spoken within the unspoken.

Emergence in the absolute does not take in conditions; this is like Yao-shan's saying, "I have a statement that has never been spoken to anyone." Tao-wu said, "They come along together." Here he understood subtly. There are many examples like this. Things must come forth in combination, without confusion of noble and base. This is called the spoken within the unspoken. Also, in reference to "I have a statement that has never been spoken to anyone," when those who engage in dialogue come forth, they must avoid rejection and attachment; both rejection and attachment are due to ignorance of what's there.

The unspoken within statements does not define nobility, does not fall into left and right; therefore it is called emergence in the absolute.

Emergence in the absolute makes it clear that the absolute is not involved in conditions. To cite more sayings, it is like "How is it when the black bean has not sprouted?" or "There is some-

one who does not breathe" or "Before conception, is there anything to say?" This is where the buddhas of the ten directions
emerge. These examples are referred to as speaking of the unspoken.

There is also borrowing phenomena for temporary use. In the
state of emergence within the absolute, the one who responds
must clarify the comprehension of things within the relative;
one cannot clarify it while plunged into the absolute state.

If you want to know how this is expressed, it is like when my
late teacher Tung-shan asked a student from Korea, "Where
were you before you crossed the sea?" There was no reply, so
Tung-shan himself said for him, " 'Right now I'm at sea, and
where am I!' "

It is also like when Tung-shan said in behalf of an elder who
held forth his staff and was asked where it came from, "It's being
held forth right now! Is there anyone who can handle it?"

In these examples, though recognition is attained within conditional objects, it is not the same as the past, when mastery
had not been attained. Later people may have relegated this to
cultivated development, considering that to be the transcendental.

For example, students pick out this saying in answer to a
question about the meaning of the founder of Zen—"I'll tell you
when a lone cow gives birth to a calf"—and say that this is
emergence within the absolute state. This kind of saying cannot
under any circumstances be considered emergence within the
absolute. It could be called dialogue on the mystic path; it's the
same thing—this is a particular path. It cannot be called integration either, because it is obvious; even if guest and host interact, it can only be called defective integration.

*There may be emergence within the relative; this is the unspoken
within the spoken.*

Emergence within the relative includes conditions, as in the saying "What can we call that which is right now?" As there was no answer, Tung-shan himself said, "Cannot but get it." There are many more such examples; this is referred to as the unspoken within the spoken.

Speech comes from elements, sound and flesh, which do not define place or direction, right or wrong. That is why it is said to be understood in relational context. This is emergence within the relative.

There are many corresponding sayings. For example, "What has come thus?" And, "When mind and objects are both forgotten, then what is this?" Also, "When concentration and insight are learned equally, you clearly see the buddha nature." These examples too, of which there are many, are referred to as the unspoken within the spoken.

Emergence within the relative is clarifying the essence within things, as in the saying "What has come thus?" and "When mind and objects are both forgotten, then what is this?" This category of saying refers to achievement to clarify state, illustrating the state in terms of the work.

Here too I used to cite corresponding examples. "What has come thus?" is one example of a saying: although it is recognized within conditions, in relational context, that is not the same as before. Also, with the example of " 'When concentration and insight are learned equally, you clearly see buddha nature'—what is this principle?" at first I would cite corresponding sayings. As for the saying "When mind and objects are both forgotten, then what is this?"—because this is an example from among the doctrines, it is not the same as mystical study. What one must do, in dealing with doctrinal examples, is to go through them into the gateway of the source. This is the exoteric side of mysticism.

In the case of the saying "Breathing out, I do not depend on conditions; breathing in, I do not abide in mental or material elements," this is all about work; it is not the same as recognition within conditions. Here too I used to cite corresponding examples of the host withdrawing into the absolute, saying, "There is someone who has no outgoing or incoming breath," to get others to know of the absolute.

There is, furthermore, an ultimate state of immaculate purity that includes work, which may also be called emergence within the relative. This is hard to discern; it must be picked out.

For example, a monk asked Tung-shan, "What is the mystic teaching?" Tung-shan replied, "Like the tongue of a dead man." Another asked, "What is presented as an offering twenty-four hours a day?" He said, "No thing." This is said to be emergence within the relative, but these two examples are not to be called emergence within the relative state. It is necessary to distinguish them individually. The saying about the "mystic teaching" could be considered the same as work and achievement, but neither saying can be referred to as the relative or as integration. It has already been made quite clear. This is using the work to illustrate the state; using the state to illustrate the work is the same as this.

There may be mutual integration: here we do not say there is the spoken or the unspoken. Here we must simply proceed directly. Here it is necessary to be perfectly fluid; things must be perfectly fluid.

With mutual integration, the force of words is neither relative nor absolute, implying neither being nor nonbeing, so they seem complete without being complete and seem lacking without lacking. One can only proceed directly; proceeding means we do not set up a goal. When they do not define a goal, words are at their most subtle. The incompleteness of the scene is a matter of ordinary sense.

An example is the saying of Tung-shan about the story of

Wen-shu and tea drinking: "Would it be possible to make use of this?" And as Ts'ui-wei said, "What do you drink every day?"

However, words on the Way are all defective; people must master spoken expressions and proceed directly ahead. The spoken is coming thus; the unspoken is going thus. Among adepts, it is not that there is no speech, but it does not get into the spoken or the unspoken. This is called integrated speech. Integrated speech has no obvious aim at all.

Integration does not fall into the spoken or the unspoken, as in Yao-shan's saying on wearing a sword, which is an integrated saying. Observe the force of the words at the moment: sometimes it is immediate and direct, and sometimes it is emptiness within differentiation. If you do not understand this subtly, you are far, far away.

To cite examples of integrated sayings, there is the saying of Wen-shu about drinking tea, and also the saying, "Where is this man gone right now?" Yun-yen said, "So what? So what?" He also said, "How about right now?" There are very many such examples.

There is also integration within work and achievement, which resembles the transcendental. It is dealt with according to the situation: for example, if you get trapped in a state of pure ethereality, then you have to realize that there are still things happening; go when you need to go, stop when you need to stop. Adapting fluidly in countless ways, do not be crude.

Now then, the forces of the words of both the one who questions and the one who replies respond to each other. None is beyond the scope of the Five Ranks. Words can be coarse or fine, however, and answers may be shallow or deep. That is why Tung-shan articulated what is not in words; in every case this was considered a necessity in response to conditions, that is all.

"People of great ignorance," being complete in essence, are not the same as "incorrigibles." "Incorrigibles" suffer mentally when they know there is something to do; yet even though they suffer mentally, they accomplish service. To suffer mentally means not to keep thinking of Zen masters, buddhas, or one's own father and mother.

"Rotten people" do not resort to total burden-bearing, so they do not set up any idol.

"People of great conservation" have got their feet stuck deeply in the mud, so maintaining their discipline is not a small matter.

Integration should be like Wen-shu's saying on drinking tea and like Tung-shan's reply to Yun-yen's ginger-digging saying, as well as Master An's saying on the teaching hall and the conversation of Yao-shan and Ch'un Pu-na on washing Buddha. For the most marveous integration of all, nothing is better than Yao-shan's answer to Tao-wu on wearing a sword, or Pai-chang's saying "What is it?" when he was leaving the hall and the congregation was about to disperse. When Yao-shan heard this saying from far away, he said, "It's here."

Integration in the darkness uses work to illuminate things, and uses things to illuminate work; it uses errors to illustrate accomplishments, and uses accomplishments to illustrate errors, equally in this way. Whatever Yao-shan, Tung-shan, and all the other worthies produced that went beyond into the absolute were just marvelous expressions of mystic conversation, that is all. When they subsequently came to those who had attained a little power, they drew them into the absolute, in which context this type of saying is commonly used.

Because I have so much to do, I haven't had the time to go into details, and have only explained a little bit. You should not slight this; if you still get frozen or stuck anywhere, you should cut through to certainty then and there. You should practice diligently, so that this thing will never be allowed to die out. Don't reveal it carelessly, but if you meet someone who is pure and simple, who is an extraordinary vessel, then it is not to be concealed.

Hung-chih

Sermons

Eᴍᴘᴛʏ ʏᴇᴛ ᴀᴡᴀʀᴇ, the original light shines spontaneously; tranquil yet responsive, the great function manifests. A wooden horse neighing in the wind does not walk the steps of the present moment; a clay ox emerging from the sea plows the springtime of the eon of emptiness.

Understand?

Where a jade man beckons, even greater marvel is on the way back.

One continuous clear void, the night precisely midway; the moon, cool, spews frost. When light and dark are merged without division, who distinguishes relative and absolute herein?

Thus it is said, "Although the absolute is absolute, yet it is relative; although the relative is relative, yet it is complete." At this precise moment, how do you discern?

How clear—twin shining eyes before any impulse!

How stately—the eternal body outside forms!

Every atom of every land is self; there is nowhere to hide. Everywhere you go, you encounter It; such a person has eyes. On the hundred grasses, at the gates of a bustling city, impossible to mix up, you do not go along with the flow; impossible to categorize, you do not leak at all.

When there is nowhere to place the mind, nothing to lean on, nothing to walk on, and nothing to say, this cannot be seen and described, cannot be grasped and manipulated. The totality of all forms is equal to its function; the whole of cosmic space is equal to its body. Ultimately free in action, it is the immortal being within species; skillfully responsive, it is in the midst of the material world, yet different.

This is why a master teacher said, "True nature is the Earth Treasury of the mind. With neither head nor tail, it develops beings according to conditions; it is provisionally referred to as knowledge." Now what is the provisional knowledge that develops beings according to conditions? Understand? "Do not think it strange how I have offered you wine over and over since we sat down, for after we part we can hardly meet again."

Standing alone and unchanging, acting comprehensively and inexhaustibly, do not disdain the phenomena filling your eyes. You must trust that in the world, which is only mental, the thousand peaks all point to the summit, and the hundred rivers all end in the sea.

If you understand in this way, you roll up the screens and remove the blinds. If you do not understand in this way, you

shut the doors and create a barrier. Whether discussing understanding or nonunderstanding, ignoramuses are not quick.

Hidden illumination inside the circle—a hibernating dragon
murmurs in the clouds enveloping withered trees. True clarity
beyond measurement—the pattern on the moon puts a soulful
face on the nocturnal orb.

The route before the shuttle can be discerned by a stone
woman; the talisman under the elbow can be used by a wooden
man. Thus all of space can be sealed with one stamp, omitting
nothing in the entire cosmos.

Understand? When the six senses convey clear meaning, the
whole world is clear of any dust.

When every particle of every land is the Self, there is no place
to hide; when one encounters It everywhere, one is endowed
with perception. Not mixed up by phenomena or swept away by
events, not susceptible to categorization, totally free from leak-
age, know that the great function manifests in the action of Zen
adepts.

One ancient master was half mad and half crazy. Another
used to sing and dance by himself. Do you understand? When
you use the wind to fan a fire, not much effort is needed. Inquire!

When the six senses return to their source, they are thoroughly
effective and clear, without compare. When the physical elements return to their source, the whole body is pure, without a

particle of dust. Thus you manage to cut off causation, interrupt its continuity, merge all time, and obliterate all differences. Understand?

> "The spiritual bird dreams on the branch that does not
> sprout;
> The flower of awakening blossoms on the tree that casts
> no shadow."

A single particle of matter involves infinite worlds; a single instant of thought transcends infinite eons. A single body manifests infinite beings; a single actuality includes infinite buddhas. This is why it is said, "Universal complete awareness is my sanctuary; body and mind live at peace in the knowlege of essential equality."

This state cannot be limited spatially or temporally. Self and other combine, merging like water and milk; center and periphery interpenetrate, reflecting each other like images in mirrors.

How do you verbalize guarding your movements to avoid harming living beings?

When there is no fluctuation from one state of mind to the next, then there is no losing direction from one step to the next.

Coming from nowhere, going nowhere, arriving at the equality of the principle of unity, we see the empty appearances of all things. Where the morning clouds have dispersed, the sun is bright; when the night rain has passed, the valley streams are swollen. The body of perception, independent, perpetually dwells on one suchness, responding to reality autonomously, a welter of myriad forms. Then you don't need to think deliberately anymore; there is naturally someone providing support to all alike.

Those of you who have attained the Great Rest: if you do not accept food, that is the fall of nobility.

Extinct without passing away, you merge consciously with space; alive without being born, you function subtly in concert with all things. Traceless before time, you are at home after embodiment. The crane dreams in its nest, cold; faintly light, there's the moon in the dark green forest. When the dragon murmurs, the night lasts long; persistent are the clouds surrounding the withered tree.

At precisely such a time, there is no birth or death, no coming or going, but there subtly exists a way to act; do you get it?

> Mist engulfs the blue-green reeds—
> snow upon the sand.
> Wind plays with the white water plants—
> autumn on the river.

The Boatman said to Chia-shan, "There should be no traces where you conceal yourself, but do not conceal yourself in the traceless. In thirty years with my teacher, I understood only this."

In the unusual grass on the cold cliff, you accomplish a task even while sitting; under the bright moon and white clouds, you emanate reflections with every step.

At just such a time, how do you act?
The recondite hollow has nothing to do
with the very idea of a lock;
What business have dualistic people
with transcendental involvement?

The clouds are naturally free, without intention; the sky is encompassing, without bounds. The Way responds universally,
without image; the spirit is always at peace, without thinking.
Follow this, and you do not see its tracks; go out to meet it, and
you do not see it coming. The whole Buddhist canon only
amounts to praises of it; the buddhas of all times can only watch
from the side.

The lamp is bright, the hall is empty; as a weaving girl oper-
ates the loom, the path of the shuttle is fine. The water is luminous, the night quiet; a fisherman clutches his reed cloak around
him, the moonlight in the boat cold.

Have you ever reached this state, this time? If not, don't bring
it up in confusion.

Pressing sesame seeds to get oil and cooking grain into cereal
are matters for graduates of Zen. In practice of the Way it is
important to be even-minded; why should it be necessary to
struggle to shift at a moment's notice?

Our livelihood is naturalness; our family way is the matter at
hand. Following the current, going along with the wind, the
homeward boat lands on the shore. Free people laugh aloud;
their mood is conveyed to those who understand.

There is not so much to Buddhism. It just requires people to make body and mind empty all the time, not wearing so much as a thread, open, relaxed, and independent, the spiritual light of the original state not being dimmed at all.

If you practice in this way, such that you attain spontaneous harmony in all places and responsiveness at all times, without the slightest thing obstructing you, so you can put all the sages behind you, only then can you be called a Zen practitioner.

If you rely on others, accepting the judgments of others and allowing yourself to be confused by others, are you not a blind ass following a crowd?

This being the case, what is it all about, after all? It's just that you don't go back; if you return, you can. Who is there to contend with in the misty waves of the lakes?

Subtle presence, profoundly calm, is not actually nothing; true perception, marvelously effective, is not actually something. Go ahead and take a step back between them and look: where the white clouds end, the green mountains are thin. Investigate!

Open purity is boundless, yet knowledge accompanies it. Universal responsiveness has no conventional method, yet the spirit is coordinated with it. When knowledge is open, it perceives spontaneously, alert and awake; the function of the spirit is continuous, without deliberate effort. Then you can radiate great light all the time everywhere, doing enlightened work.

This is why it is said, "Mountains and rivers present no barrier; light penetrates everywhere." And haven't you read the saying "If people want to enter the realm of buddhas, they should make their minds clear as space, detaching from all appearances and fixations, causing the mind to be unobstructed where it turns"?

> How do you act so as to attain this union?
> Water and moon, calm, face one another;
> The breeze in the pines, clear, has never stopped.

Why is it that those who have swallowed the buddhas of all times cannot open their mouths? Why is it that those who have seen through the whole world cannot close their eyes?

I have removed many sicknesses for you all at once; but how can you get completely well? Understand? Breaking open the colors of Flower Mountain range soaring to the sky, releasing the sound of the Yellow River reaching the sea.

If the host does not know there is a guest, then there is no way to respond to the world; if the guest does not know there is a host, then there is no vision beyond material senses.

How is someone who has gone? Utterly silent, without a trace. How about someone who has come back? Perfectly clear; something is going on.

Dig the pond, don't wait for the moonlight; when the pond is complete, the moonlight will naturally be there.

In ephemeral objects, past, present, and future move from renewal to renewal. Within solid earth, initial positive energy
subtly sprouts into movement. Sojourning without dwelling,
one unobtrusively turns the wheel of potential; alive without
birth, one ineffably transcends illusory phenomena.

This is how we borrow space for our body and use everything
for our function, responding to the invitation of the whole world
without stress, fully comprehending the void within the stamp
of unity without exclusion.

But how do you experientially comprehend life without birth?
Understand?

> If you want to know what will happen in spring,
> The winter plum blossoms simply do not know.

Every flame of the eonic fire is an ember of events; in the emptiness of the eonic void there is a pedestal of awareness. There is
no more beauty and ugliness to make flaws; beauty and ugliness
both come from here.

By the forms of combinations of objects and mind, puppets act
out their parts on a stage. Breaking through the painted screen,
come on back; the home fields are broad and clear.

Use the light of the origin to wash away the darkness of the
long night of ignorance; use the knowledge of the cosmos to

break through the doubts of countless eons. Birth and death go on in profusion, but they do not reach the house of true purity; entangling conditions are troublesome, but they do not reach the realm of complete clarity. Let them change outside, while you as an individual remain empty within. Walking into the circle of the Way, you comprehend and forget illusory phenomena.

This is why an ancient said, "There is something before the universe; formless, originally quiescent, it is the master of myriad forms, never withering through the four seasons."

> But tell me, what is this?
> A whale drinks up the ocean water,
> Exposing the coral branches.

White is colorless, but it is placed before all colors; water is flavorless, yet all flavors are best with it. The Way has no root, but it pervades the universe; the Teaching has no fixed form, and can be this or that. A valley is always empty, but the echo can answer a call; a mirror is itself clear, while the reflections correspond to forms.

If you really attain such a body and mind, your great function, completely free, cannot be exploited. But tell me, who is it that cannot be exploited?

Understand?

Subtly transcending at the incipience of thought, standing independent before myriad impulses.

The body is not a collection of atoms but a stately, wondrous being. The mind is not emotional and intellectual entanglements but an unknowable solitary awareness.

The substance is beyond all obstruction. The function is very independent. No going or coming, neither obvious nor occult, response to form and sound are void of opposition or dependence.

The saving grace in the cakes and cookies is up to us members of the guild doing our business.

When rich in myriad virtues, even if ephemeral things are very prominent, you are entirely clear of dust.

Deliberately stopping speech and thought to plunge absolutely into tranquil silence, your inner way of being spontaneously shines, and you roam independent in the realm of true eternity.

When you take it up, it is crystal clear; a thousand differences and ten thousand distinctions cannot mix it up. When you put it down, it is free of all attributes; no trace can be found in any place or any time.

This is why ancients spoke of being impossible to trap, impossible to call back, not categorized even by the ancient sages, having no fixed place even now.

But tell me, how does one behave in order to attain such a realization?

Do you comprehend?

"Walking to where the stream ends, sitting and watching when the clouds arise."

When people are even, they do not speak; when water is level, it does not flow. When the wind is calm, flowers still fall; when birds sing, the mountains seem even deeper.

Thus natural reality has no lack or excess; don't interpolate anything at all.

In the realm of purity and coolness, the whole container of fresh air is steeped in autumn. When body and mind are clarified, the misty face of midnight embraces the moon. Spirituality spontaneous, open and always empty, you cut off the conditioning of birth and death and depart from subjective evaluations of what is and what is not.

Have you reached such a state, and are you capable of behaving in such a manner?

"When you have felled the cassia tree on the moon,
The pure light must be even more."

Truly arrive at the emptiness of time, and you understand yourself; when you do not fall into being or nonbeing, you transcend birth and death.

The night boat, carrying the moon, fishes the river of freedom; the heritage of pure clarity is just like this.

Affection congeals to form the body; thoughts settle to form the world; henceforth you bob around in the sea of birth and death.

When you see through to the spiritual source, whose profound stillness is unmixed, then you will know that illusions and bubbles present no obstacle.

When the weather is autumn in the senses and the conditions

of the gross elements disintegrate, one reality always remains, with perfect clarity.

Merged in the bright moonlight, the snow and reeds are confusing to the eye; sent by a pure breeze, the night boat's return is swift.

Color empties, thus taking up the seal of the lineage of buddhas and Zen masters; light dissolves darkness, perpetuating the lamp that illumines the world.

At this time you do not fall into thought; in this situation you can, however, turn freely.

This is why the Boatman said, "Let there be no traces where you hide, but do not hide where there are no traces. In thirty years with Yao-shan, I understood only this."

Now tell me, what was understood? Do you comprehend?

The tortoise returns to its ocean palace; the evening tide recedes; as the moon passes the river of stars, the soul of the night is clear.

Intellect open and luminous, spirit calm and penetrating, clear cold transforms the night; a frosty moon traverses the sky.

This is how a Zen practitioner should behave, the four quarters and eight directions all crystal clear. Investigate!

Empty, empty, absolutely trackless, not dimmed by even a dot; when profoundly still, free from words, unified potential spontaneously goes into operation.

At this point even the past and future buddhas do not presume to claim teacherhood; at this point even the founders of Zen do not claim to be masters.

Understand?

> The golden needle is under double lock;
> The road of harmonization is subtly all-inclusive.

Magnificent, distinguished, it is revealed uniquely in myriad forms; clear, evident, it is encountered in all things. I do not see any external other; the other does not see any external me. Other is not outside of self, so objects of sense vanish; self is not outside of other, so feelings of perception are shed.

This is why it is said, "The world is thus, beings are thus; every particle is thus, and every thought is thus."

But tell me, how does one act so as to attain such a realization? Understand?

> Unified potential subtly operating, the hub of the Way
>   is still;
> Myriad images' reflections flowing, the mind mirror
>   is empty.

The House of
YUN-MEN

Hsueh-feng

Sayings

The whole universe, the whole world, is you; do you think there is any other? This is why the *Heroic Progress Scripture* says, "People lose themselves, pursuing things; if they could turn things around, they would be the same as Buddha."

You must perceive your essential nature before you attain enlightenment. What is perceiving essential nature? It means perceiving your own original nature.

What is its form? When you perceive your own original nature, there is no concrete object to see.

This is hard to believe in, but all buddhas achieve it.

Terms for the one mind are buddha nature, true suchness, the hidden essence, the pure spiritual body, the pedestal of awareness, the true soul, the innocent, universal mirrorlike cognition, the empty source, the ultimate truth, and pure consciousness.

The buddhas of past, present, and future, and all of their

scriptural discourses, are all in your original nature, inherently complete. You do not need to seek, but you must save yourself. No one can do it for you.

Look, look at these grown-ups traveling to the ends of the earth! Wherever you go, when someone asks you what the matter is, you immediately say hello, say good-bye, raise your eyebrows, roll your eyes, step forward, and withdraw. Broadcasting this sort of bad breath, the minute you get started you enter a wild fox cave. Taking the servant for the master, you do not know pollution from purity. Deceiving yourselves in the present, at the end of your lives you will turn out to be nothing more than a bunch of wild foxes.

Do you understand? How does this produce good people? Having received the shelter of Shakyamuni Buddha, you destroy his sacred heritage. What kind of attitude is this? All over China, Buddhism is dying out right before our eyes. Don't think this is an idle matter! As I sit here, I do not see a single individual who qualifies as an initiate in the Zen message of time immemorial. You are just a random collection, a gang ruining Buddhism. The ancients would call you people who repudiate wisdom. You will have to reject this before you can attain realization.

To attain this matter requires strength of character; don't keep on running to me over and over again, depending on me, seeking statements and asking for sayings. For a man of the required character, that is making fools of people. Do you know good from bad? I'll have to chase this bunch of ignoramuses away with my cane!

If you immediately realize being-so, that is best and most economical; don't let yourself come to me for a statement. Understand? If you are a descendant of the founder of Zen, you will not eat food that another has already chewed.

What is more, you should not cramp yourself. Right now, what do you lack? The business of the responsible individual has been as clear as the bright sun in the blue sky for all time. There has never been anything at all obstructing it; so why don't you know it?

If I were to tell you that in order to understand you would have to take half a step, to exercise the slightest bit of effort, to read a single word of scripture, or to explicitly ask questions of others, I would be deceiving and threatening you.

What is this right here and now?

Unable to get it, and also unable to step back into yourself and examine thoroughly to see for yourself, you only know to go to ignorant and muddle-headed "old teachers" to memorize sayings. What relevance is there? Do you know this is not something verbal? I tell you, if you memorize a single phrase of a saying, you'll be a wild fox sprite for all time. Do you understand?

YUN-MEN
Sayings

THE OPPORTUNITY to preach the Way is certainly hard to handle; even if you accord with it in a single saying, this is still fragmentation. If you go on at random, that is even more useless.

Now then, there are divisions within the vehicles of the Teaching: the precepts are for moral studies, the scriptures are for learning concentration, and the treatises are for learning wisdom. The Three Baskets, Five Vehicles, Five Times, and Eight Teachings each have their goal. But even if you directly understand the complete immediate teaching of the One Vehicle, which is so hard to understand, this is still far from Zen realization.

In Zen, even if you present your state in a phrase, this is still uselessly bothering to tarry in thought. Zen methods, with their interactive techniques, have countless variations and differences; if you try to get ahead, your mistake lies in pursuing the expressions of others.

What about the perennial concern? Can you call this complete, can you call it immediate? Can you call it mundane or transcendental? Better not misconstrue this! When you hear me speaking this way, do not immediately turn to where there is neither completeness nor immediateness to figure and calculate.

Here, it is necessary for you to be the one to realize it; do not present sayings from a teacher, imitation sayings, or calculated sayings everywhere you go, making them out to be your own understanding.

Do not misunderstand. Right now, what is the matter?

Better not say I'm fooling you today. To begin with, I have no choice but to make a fuss in front of you, but if I were seen by someone with clear eyes, I'd be a laughingstock. Right now I can't avoid it, so let me ask you all: What has ever been the matter? What do you lack?

Even if I tell you there's nothing the matter, I've already buried you, and yet you must arrive at this state before you will realize it. And don't run off at the mouth asking questions at random; as long as your own mind is unclear, you still have a lot of work to do in the future.

If your faculties and thoughts work slowly, then for now examine the methods and techniques set up by the ancients, to see what their principles are.

Do you want to attain understanding? The subjective ideas you yourself have been entertaining for measureless eons are so dense and thick that when you hear someone giving an explanation, you immediately conceive doubts and ask about the Buddha, ask about the Teaching, ask about transcendence, ask about accommodation. As you seek understanding, you become further estranged from it.

You miss it the moment you try to set your mind on it; how much more so when you talk! Would that mean that not trying to set the mind on it is right? What else is the matter? Take care!

If I were to bring up a single saying that enabled you to attain understanding immediately, this would already be scattering filth on your heads. Even if you understand the whole world all at once when a single hair is picked up, this is gouging out flesh and making a wound. Nevertheless, you must actually arrive at this state before you realize this. If you have not, then don't try to fake it in the meantime.

What you must do is step back and figure out your own standpoint: what logic is there to it?

There really is nothing at all to give you to understand, or to give you to wonder about, because each of you has your own business. When the great function appears, it does not take any effort on your part; now you are no different from the Zen masters and buddhas. It's just that your roots of faith are shallow and thin, while your bad habits are dense and thick.

Suddenly you get all excited and go on long journeys with your bowls and bags; why do you undergo such inconvenience? What insufficiency is there in you? You are adults; who has no lot? Even when you attain understanding individually on your own, this is still not being on top of things; so you shouldn't accept the deceptions of others or the judgments of others.

The minute you see some old monk open his mouth, you should shut him right up. Instead you act like green flies on a pile of manure, struggling to consume it. Gathering together in groups for discussion, you bore others miserably.

The ancients would utter a saying or half a statement for particular occasions, because of the helplessness of people like you, in order to open up ways of entry for you. If you know this, put them to one side and apply a bit of your own power; haven't you a little familiarity?

Alas, time does not wait for anyone; when you breathe out, there's no guarantee you'll breathe in again. What other body and mind do you have to employ at leisure somewhere else? You simply must pay attention! Take care.

Take the whole universe all at once and put it on your eyelashes.

When you hear me talk this way, you might come up excitedly and give me a slap, but relax for now and examine carefully the question of whether such a thing exists or not and what it means.

Even if you understand this, if you run into a member of a Zen school you'll probably get your legs broken.

If you are an independent individual, when you hear someone say that an old adept is teaching somewhere, you will spit right in that person's face for polluting your ears and eyes.

If you do not have this ability, as soon as you hear someone mention something like this, you will immediately accept it, so that you have already fallen into the secondary. Don't you see how Master Te-shan used to haul out his staff the moment he saw monks enter his gate, and chase them out? When Master Mu-chou saw monks come through his gate, he would say, "The issue is at hand; I ought to give you a thrashing!"

How about the rest? The general run of thieving phonies eat up the spit of other people, memorizing a bunch of trash, a load of garbage, then running off at the mouth like asses wherever they go, boasting that they can pose questions on five or ten sayings. Even if you can pose questions from morning till night and give answers from night till morning, on until the end of time, will you ever even dream of seeing? Where is the empowerment for people? Whenever someone gives a feast for Zen monks, people like this also say they've gotten food to eat. How are they worth talking to? Someday, in the presence of death, your verbal explanations will not be accepted.

One who has attained may spend the days following the group in another's house, but if you have not attained, don't be a faker! It will not do to pass the time taking it easy; you should be most thoroughly attentive.

The ancients had a lot of complex ways of helping out. For example, Master Hsueh-feng said, "The whole earth is you!" Master Chia-shan said, "Find me in the hundred grasses; recognize the emperor in the bustling marketplace." Luo-p'u said, "As soon as a single atom comes into existence, the whole earth is contained within it. There's a lion in every hair, and this is true of the whole body." Take these up and think them over, again and again; eventually, after a long, long time, you will naturally find a way to penetrate.

No one can do this task for you; it is up to each individual alone. The old masters who emerge in the world just act as witnesses to your understanding. If you have penetrated, a little bit of reasoning won't confuse you; if you have really not attained yet, then even the use of expedients to stimulate you won't work.

All of you have worn out footgear traveling around, having left your mentors and elders, your fathers and mothers. You must apply some perceptive power before you will attain realization. If you have no penetration, if you should run into someone with really effective methods who ungrudgingly devotes life to going into the mud and water to help others, someone who is worth associating with and who disrupts complacency, then hang up your bowls and bags for ten or twenty years to attain penetration.

Don't worry that you might not succeed, because even if you don't get it in the present life, you will still not lose your humanity in the future life. Thus you will also save energy in this quest; you will not betray your whole life in vain, nor will you betray those who supported you, your mentors and elders, your fathers and mothers.

You must be attentive. Don't waste time traveling around the countryside, passing a winter here and a summer there, enjoying the landscape, seeking enjoyment, plenty of food, and readily available clothing and utensils. What a pain! Counting on that peck of rice, you lose six months' provisions. What is the benefit in journeys like this? How can you digest even a single vegetable leaf, or even a grain of rice, given by credulous almsgivers?

You must see for yourself that there is no one to substitute for you, and time does not wait for anyone. One day the light of your eyes will fall to the ground; how can you prevent that from happening? Do not be like lobsters dropped in boiling water, hands and feet thrashing. There will be no room for you to be fakers talking big talk.

Don't waste the time idly. Once you have lost humanity, you can never restore it. This is not a small matter. Do not rely on the immediate present. Even a worldly man said, "If you hear the Way in the morning, it would be all right to die that night"—then what about ascetics like us—what should we practice? You should really be diligent. Take care.

It is obvious that the times are decadent; we are at the tail end of the age of imitation. These days monks go north saying they are going to bow to Manjushri and go south saying they are going to visit Mount Heng. Those who go on journeys like this are mendicants only in name, vainly consuming the alms of the credulous.

What a pain! When you ask them a question, they are totally in the dark. They just pass the days suiting their temperament. If there are some of you who have mislearned a lot, memorizing manners of speech, seeking similar sayings wherever you go for the approval of the elder residents, slighting the high-minded, acting in ways that spiritually impoverish you, then do not say, when death comes knocking at your door, that no one told you.

If you are a beginner, you should activate your spirit and not vainly memorize sayings. A lot of falsehood is not as good as a little truth; ultimately you will only cheat yourself.

MING-CHIAO
Essays

THAT WHICH HAS FORM emerges from that which has no form; that which has no form emerges from that which has form. Therefore the path of supreme spirituality cannot be sought in being and cannot be fathomed in nonbeing; it cannot be lost through movement and cannot be gained through stillness.

Is the path of sages empty? Then where does continual renewal of life come from? Is the path of sages not empty? What lives that does not die? To accurately comprehend both emptiness and nonemptiness in the path of sages would be desirable.

Now then, to prove emptiness experientially, there is nothing better than to understand that which has form. To understand that which has form, there is nothing better than to know that which has no form. If you know that which has no form, then you can see into the light of the spirit. When you can see into the light of the spirit, then you can talk about the path.

The path is where the spirit develops, and it is where consciousness comes from. Consciousness is a source of great problems. To say that the path of the sages is empty is to sink into a void of diffuseness, so that sickness becomes even sicker. Who in the world can cure this?

The teaching of sages is in the path. The path of the sages is in awakening. Awakening means enlightenment; not awakening means not being enlightened. Not being enlightened is what separates the majority of consciousnesses from sagehood.

Awakening does not mean gradually waking up; it means being completely awake. Complete awakening is the consummation of the task of sages. Being awake is called buddhahood; it is likened to a vehicle. By awakening, one completes the path of sages; by this vehicle one reaches the realm of sages. This is true of all sages, past and future.

The awakening of sages lies within the normal awareness of ordinary people, but ordinary people wake up every day without ever realizing it. Even though they are awake, they are still dreaming; even though aware, they are still muddled. That is why the sages took the trouble to point it out to them, hoping that they'd seek awakening, inducing them to head for it, hoping they would attain it.

Contemplating the mind is called the path; elucidating the path is called education. Education is the trail left by the sages; the path is the universal root of all living beings.

People have long misunderstood the root seriously; if sages did nothing about it, everyone would end up ignorant. That is why the sages have given people great illumination.

The mind has no outside, and the path has no inside, so there is no one who is not on the path. Sages are not selfish; the path does not abandon people; sages give everything that the path involves. Therefore their education penetrates both darkness and light, both the mundane and the transmundane; nothing is not penetrated.

Penetration means unification. Unification is a means of rectification, so that everyone will have the same virtues as sages.

For universal spiritual enlightenment, the path is supreme; for subtle functions of spiritual powers, the mind is supreme. When it comes to pursuing illusions and binding activities, nothing is worse that missing the root. When it comes to wandering in mundane routines, nothing is worse than death and rebirth. When it comes to recognizing the faults and ills of ordinary people, no one is more skilled than sages. When it comes to straightening the basis for all people, nothing is better than establishing education.

When correctness is stable, there is illumination. When illumination is stable, there is sublimation. When sublimation is stable, the path is consummated therein.

Therefore education is the great beginning of the sages' illumination of the path to save the world. Education is the inconceivable great function by which sages take advantage of timely opportunities to respond to potentials.

So it is that people of great potential go the immediate way, while those of lesser potential go the gradual way. The gradual way refers to the provisional; the immediate way refers to the real. The real is called the Great Vehicle, the provisional is called the Lesser Vehicle. The sages disseminated the great and the small among people of all kinds of potentials, so darkness and light were comprehended.

Hearing the immediate in the gradual teaching or hearing the gradual in the immediate teaching are also ways in which sages are more subtle than angels or humans and unfathomable to angels or humans. Sages teach the provisional to induce people to head for the real; sages illustrate the real so that people will avail themselves of the provisional. Therefore the provisional and the real, the partial and the complete, always concern one another.

Within the provisional, there is the manifest provisional and the hidden provisional. Sages' use of the manifest provisional

involves shallow teaching, a small path, to provide a small resting place for believers. Sages' use of the hidden provisional involves other paths, other teachings, cooperating with the good
and the bad, to provide nonbelievers with remote conditions for
attaining enlightenment. The manifest provisional is obvious,
but the hidden provisional is unfathomable.

As for the real, it is final truth. In the reality of final truth,
others and self are one. Because others and self are one, sages
are such because of all beings.

If we talk about the provisional teaching of sages, it would
seem to be the great expediency that pervades all the goodness
in the world, all the paths of the philosophers, for saving the
world and helping people out. If we talk about the real teaching
of sages, it would seem to be the universal path that pervades
the universe and limits all things, finding out the truth and fulfilling nature for all the world.

As for sages, their sagacity is in not dying or being reborn
yet showing death and showing birth, the same as other people,
without anyone seeing why it is so. This does not only mean
people of ancient times with highly developed spirituality and
knowledge. That is why their education includes the spirit way
as well as the human way; there are ordinary virtues, and there
are extraordinary virtues—it is impossible to fit everything into
one generalization, and this cannot be discussed in the same
terms as worldly ways. Attainment lies in mental penetration;
loss lies in comparison of traces.

Feelings emerge from nature, whereas nature is concealed in
feelings. When nature is concealed, the path of ultimate reality
is inoperative. That is why sages use nature for their teaching
to educate people.

Activities and movements in society start from feelings. The confusions of the masses are rectified by nature. How can society not examine the positive and negative aspects of feelings and nature? They know good and bad but not how good and bad begin and end; is that complete knowledge? Is it complete knowledge to know the end but not the beginning?

Only the consummate knowledge of sages knows the beginning and the end, knows the subtle and the nonexistent, and sees what pervades death and birth, dark and light, and makes images and forms.

The world is most extensive, but it arises from feelings. The universe is most enormous, yet it is contained within nature. Therefore nothing is more powerful than feeling and nature.

Feeling is the beginning of being. When there is being, then there is affection. When there is affection, then there is desire. When there is desire, then men, women, and all beings are born and die therein.

The experiences of death and life, good and bad, typically change; they begin and they end, cyclically passing away and regenerating unceasingly.

Nature is the attainment of nonbeing. Ultimate nonbeing does not mean nonexistence; it emerges at birth and submerges at death, without itself dying or being born.

The reason for the tranquillity of the path of sages is obvious: they only sense what is suitable.

Now then, feeling is artifice, and it is consciousness; when you have it, that makes for affection, sympathy, intimacy. But intimacy makes distance, and distance makes for inconsistent good and ill.

When you lose feeling, that makes for cheating, for cunning, for viciousness, for unruliness, for greed, for addiction, for loss of mind and destruction of nature.

As for nature, it is reality, it is suchness, it is perfection, it is innocence, it is purity, it is serenity. When you get near it, you become wise and upright. In the near term, it makes people decent and upright; in the long run, it makes sanctified spirits and great sages. This is what underlies the fact that sages educate people with teaching about nature, not feeling.

Feeling and nature exist in beings always, as ever. When you try to find them out, you cannot grasp them; even if you try to cut them off, they do not end. Sky and earth have an end, but the soul of nature does not die out.

Different states of mundane existence may alternate and change, but the burden of feeling does not dissolve. Therefore society has to distinguish between the meanings of feeling and nature. If people are educated on the basis of feeling, they remain within birth and death. If people are educated on the basis of nature, they get beyond death and birth. The education of feeling is short-ranged; the education of nature is long-ranged. If you pretend to be beyond death and rebirth and take a nihilistic view of them, then you are ignorant of the pattern of nature and you cut off the source of continual regeneration.

Small knowledge cannot reach great knowledge; the final destination of a game hen is the cooking pot, is it not?

When the mind stirs, that is called activity. Coordinated activity is called experience. Experience refers to both the internal and the external. Whose mind does not stir? Who does not experience the activities of myriad beings? The pattern of activity is recondite; the momentum of experience is far reaching. Therefore people do not notice and do not fear. The education of sages is to be careful of activity, so people will be on the alert, so that they will beware of stirring in the mind.

Internal experiencing is called beckoning, and external experiencing is called response. Beckoning is considered the cause; response is considered the result. The concrete and abstract forms of cause and effect are all involved.

Now then, movement in the mind may be perverse, or it may be harmonious; this is why good and bad feelings arise therein. Once good and bad feelings occur, then calamity and fortune come in response. To the degree that feelings are more or less shallow or deep, the consequences are more or less light or heavy. The light may be shifted, but the heavy cannot be removed.

Good and bad may precede or follow; calamity and fortune may be slow or swift. Even after ten generations, or even ten thousand generations, it is impossible to escape experiencing consequences. It is not only a matter of just one generation. Those who doubt this just because good and bad do not show results in one generation are ignorant of causality.

If rewards are not based on correct causality, then how can good people be encouraged in society? We do not see trees growing, yet they flourish day by day; we do not see a whetstone wearing down, yet it diminishes day by day. That is how it is with human actions, so how can we not be careful?

HSUEH-TOU

Stories

Te-shan Guides the Crowd

TE-SHAN SAID to a group, "Tonight I won't answer any questions. Anyone who asks a question gets a thrashing."

At that point, a monk came forward and bowed, whereupon Te-shan hit him.

The monk said, "I haven't even asked a question yet!"

Te-shan said, "Where are you from?"

The monk said, "Korea."

Te-shan said, "You deserved a thrashing before you stepped on the boat!"

Fa-yen brought this up and said, "The great Te-shan's talk is dualistic."

Yuan-ming brought this up and said, "The great Te-shan has a dragon's head but a snake's tail."

Hsueh-tou brought this up and commented, "Though the old masters Fa-yen and Yuan-ming skillfully trimmed the long and added to the short, gave up the heavy and went along with the light, this is not enough to see Te-shan.

"Why? Te-shan was as if holding the authority outside the

118

door; he had a sword that would not invite disorder even when he didn't cut off when he should.

"Do you want to see the Korean monk? He is just a blind fellow bumping into a pillar."

Pai-chang and the Whisk

Pai-chang called on Ma-tsu a second time and stood there, attentive. Ma-tsu stared at the whisk on the edge of his seat.

Pai-chang asked, "Does one identify with this function or detach from this function?"

Ma-tsu said, "Later on, when you open your lips, what will you use to help people?"

Pai-chang picked up the whisk and held it up.

Ma-tsu said, "Do you identify with this function or detach from this function?"

Pai-chang hung the whisk back in its place.

Ma-tsu then shouted, so loudly that Pai-chang was deaf for three days.

Hsueh-tou brought this up and said, "Extraordinary, O Zen worthies! Nowadays, those who branch off in streams are very many, while those who search out the source are extremely few. Everyone says that Pai-chang was greatly enlightened at the shout, but is it really true or not?

"Similar ideographs resemble each other and get mixed up, but clear-eyed people couldn't be fooled one bit. When Ma-tsu said, 'Later on, when you open your lips, what will you use to help people?' Pai-chang held up the whisk—do you consider this to be like insects chewing wood, accidentally making a pattern, or is it breaking out of and crashing into a shell at the same time?

"Do you want to understand the three days of deafness? Pure gold, highly refined, should not change in color."

Hsueh-feng's Ancient Stream

A monk asked Hsueh-feng, "How is it when the ancient stream is cold from the source?"

Hsueh-feng said, "When you look directly into it, you don't see the bottom."

The monk asked, "How about one who drinks of it?"

Hsueh-feng said, "It doesn't go in by way of the mouth."

The monk recounted this to Chao-chou. Chao-chou said, "It can't go in by way of the nostrils."

The monk then asked Chao-chou, "How is it when the ancient stream is cold from the source?"

Chao-chou said, "Painful."

The monk said, "What about one who drinks of it?"

Chao-chou said, "He dies."

Hsueh-feng heard this quoted and said, "Chao-chou is an ancient buddha; from now on, I won't answer any more questions."

Hsueh-tou brought this up and commented, "Everyone in the crowd says that Hsueh-feng didn't go beyond this monk's question, and that is why Chao-chou didn't agree. If you understand literally in this way, you'll deeply disappoint the ancients.

"I dissent. Only one who can cut nails and shear iron is a real Zen master. Going to the low, leveling the high, one could hardly be called an adept."

Ts'ao-shu and the Nation of Han

Ts'ao-shu asked a monk, "Where have you recently come from?"

The monk said, "The nation of Han."

Ts'ao-shu asked, "Does the emperor of Han respect Buddhism?"

The monk said, "How miserable! Lucky you asked me! Had you asked another, there would have been a disaster!"

Ts'ao-shu asked, "What are you doing?"

The monk said, "I don't even see people's existence—what Buddhism is there to respect?"

Ts'ao-shu asked, "How long have you been ordained?"

The monk said, "Twenty years."

Ts'ao-shu said, "A fine 'not seeing people's existence'!" And he hit him.

Hsueh-tou commented, "This monk took a beating, but when he goes he won't return. As for Ts'ao-shu, while he carried out the imperative, he roused waves where there was no wind."

The House of
FA-YEN

Hsuan-sha
Sayings

Have you attained the pure, original ocean of insight and knowledge of essence and forms? If you haven't attained it yet, now that you are gathered here, do you see the green mountains before you? If you say you see, how do you see? If you say you do not see, how can you say the green mountains are not visible? Do you understand?

The fact is that your pure, original ocean of insight and knowledge of essence and forms includes seeing and hearing. If you understand, it is just so, and even if you don't understand, it is still just so.

Everything is always so; every essence is as such; just do not seek outside. If you have a great root of faith, then the buddhas are nothing but your own inner experience; whether you are walking, standing still, sitting, or reclining, never is it not so.

But now that I've told you this directly, already I am oppressing your freedom, making you slaves. Would you agree to say so? Whether you agree or not, how do you understand?

Now this talk is already showing ignorance of good and bad. How so? Because you discriminate this way and that way.

What are you all taking such pains in search of? Don't tell me to flap my lips! Why? There is nothing accomplished by talk alone; it is not words that can bring people peace. You must experience unity and suchness before you attain harmony; don't just memorize sayings and expressions, for there is no end to that. It's just a matter of total concentration. Don't say you have to attain the function of the sages before you can be free; how are you unequal to them?

The emergence of buddhas in the world exercising kindness and compassion has been all along like flowers in the sky, without solid reality. You should realize that there is that which has never emerged in the world and has never entered extinction.

Illusory manifestations and illusory names have no reality. Why? The essential nature of the material elements is fundamentally actually empty, so it has never passed away and never come to be, and it has never taught people.

Because the essential nature of beings is such, their material bodies are also such. Because the essential nature of beings is nirvanic, their material bodies are also nirvanic. But do you realize this?

If you do, then come forth and we'll all discuss it. If not, I now tell you that intrinsic essence does not produce intrinsic essence, and intrinsic essence does not annihilate intrinsic essence.

Then how can one attain understanding? Don't say this essential nature is as ever. If you understand, please express your understanding to the people; if you do not understand, then how are you not comparable to the buddhas?

This is how you must be before you attain. Those of higher faculties comprehend everything once they hear; those of middling faculties also comprehend once they hear; and those of lesser faculties also comprehend once they hear. What am I talking about with this reasoning? Do you know? Do you have insight?

It is inherent in everyone; it is manifest in everyone.

The first axiom of Zen is to personally accept the completeness of present actuality. There is no other in the whole universe; it is just you. Who else would you have see? Who would you have hear? All of it is the doing of your mind monarch, fulfilling immutable knowledge. All you lack is personal acceptance of the realization. This is called opening the door of expedient methodology, to get you to trust that there is a flow of true eternity that pervades all time. There's nothing that is not it and nothing that is it.

This axiom only amounts to equanimity. Why? It is just using words to dismiss words, using principle to chase principle, teaching people equilibrium and constancy in essence and in manifestation for their own benefit. In terms of Zen, this is still understanding what comes before but not understanding what comes afterward. This is called uniform ordinariness, the experience of partial realization of the body of reality.

Without expression beyond patterns, you die at the statement and do not yet have any freedom. If you know experience beyond patterns, you will not be compelled by mental demons; they come within your power, and you can transform them effortlessly. Your words communicate the great Way, without falling into the view of even-mindedness. This is called the first axiom of Zen.

The second axiom is returning to causality and attending to effects, not sticking to the principle of constant oneness. This is expediently called turning from state to potential, enlivening and killing freely, granting and taking away as appropriate, emerging in life and entering in death, bringing benefits to all. Transcendently free of material desires and emotional views, this is expediently called the buddha nature that goes beyond the whole world all at once. This is called simultaneous understanding of two principles, equal illumination of two truths. Unmoved by dualistic extremism, subtle functions become manifest. This is called the second axiom of Zen.

The third axiom is to know that there is a root source of the nature and characteristics of great knowledge and to penetrate its infinite vision, understanding both the negative and the positive, comprehending the universe. The enhanced function of the one real essential nature becomes manifest, responding to developments without convention. Functioning completely without any effort, totally alive without any initiative, this is expediently called the method of concentration of compassion. This is the third axiom of Zen.

KUEI-CH'EN
Sayings

Don't lower your heads and think; thought cannot reach. If you then say you did not need to be discerning, do you understand enough to express it in words? Where will you begin your speech? Try to tell.

Is there anything that can get you nearer? Is there anything that can get you farther? Is there anything that can make you the same? Is there anything that can make you different? Then why do you particularly go to so much trouble? It is because you are weak and lack character, fretfully guarding the conceptual faculty, afraid that people will question you.

I always say, if you have any enlightenment, then reveal it without any sense of others or self; I will check it for you.

Why do you not accept what is right at hand? Don't take a puddle for an ocean. Buddhism pervades the universe; don't make the mistake of subjectively defining knowledge and views in your little heart and drawing the boundaries there. This is perception and cognition, thought and feeling. And yet it is not that this is wrong; but if you nod here and say you've found true reality, then you don't get it.

Now what about the ancient saying "Only I can know"—what perspective is this? Do you know? Is it not, "You see me,

I see you"? Don't misunderstand! If it were this self, the self goes along with birth and death: as long as the body exists, it is there; but when the body is no longer, it is not there. That is why the ancient buddhas said, for the sake of you people of today, difference produces differences; when there is no difference, differences disappear.

Don't take this lightly; the matter of birth and death is serious. If you don't evaporate this mass, there will be plenty of discord wherever you are; if you don't break through sound and form, the same will be so of sensation, perception, conditioning, and consciousness. Even if your bones are sticking out, don't say that the five clusters are originally void. It does not depend on your claim to have understood emptiness. That is why it is said that you must personally attain penetration, and you have to be genuinely authentic.

I am not the first one to talk like this. The ancient sages have informed you of what they called the indestructible esoteric treasury of inconceivable light. It covers the whole universe, giving birth to the ordinary and nurturing the saintly, pervading all time. Who has none of it? Then who would you depend on anymore?

Thus the buddhas, in their compassion, seeing you helpless, opened up the door of expedient methodology, pointing out the characteristics of true reality. Now I am using expedient method; do you understand? If you do not understand, don't make up wonders in your conceptual faculty.

FA-YEN

Ten Guidelines for Zen Schools

Author's Own Preface

I SHED THE CAGE of entanglements in youth and grew up hearing the essentials of the Teaching, traveling around calling on teachers for nearly thirty years. The Zen schools, in particular, are widespread, most numerous in the South. Yet few in them have arrived at attainment; such people are rarely found.

Anyway, even though noumenal principle is a matter for sudden understanding, actualities must be realized gradually. The teaching methods of the schools have many techniques, of course, but insofar as they are for dealing with people for their benefit, the ultimate aim is the same.

If, however, people have no experience of the doctrines of the teachings, it is hard to break through discrimination and subjectivity. Galloping right views over wrong roads, mixing inconsistencies into important meanings, they delude people of the following generations and inanely enter into vicious circles.

I have taken the measure of this, and it is quite deep; I have made the effort to get rid of it, but I have not fully succeeded. The mentality that blocks the tracks just grows stronger; the intellectual undercurrent is not useful.

Where there are no words, I forcefully speak out; where there is no dogma, I strongly uphold certain principles. Pointing out defects in Zen schools, I briefly explain ten matters, using words critical of specific errors to rescue an era from decadence.

1. On False Assumption of Teacherhood Without Having Cleared One's Own Mind Ground

The teaching of the mind ground is the basis of Zen study. What is the mind ground? It is the great awareness of those who arrive at suchness.

From no beginning, a moment of confusion mistaking things for oneself, craving and desire flare up, and you flow in the waves of birth and death. The radiance of awareness is dimmed, covered up by ignorance; routines of behavior push you on, so you cannot be free.

Once you have lost human status, you cannot restore it. That is why the buddhas emerged in the world with so many expedient methods; if you get stuck on expressions and pursue words, you will fall back into eternalism or nihilism. Through the compassion of the Zen masters, the mind seal was communicated unalloyed, so that people could transcend the ordinary and the sacred at once, without going through stages; it just got them to awaken on their own and sever the root of doubt forever.

People of recent times take a lot lightly. They may enter communes, but they are lazy about pursuing intense inquiry. Even if they develop concentration, they do not select a true master; through the mistakes of false teachers, like them they lose direction to the ultimate. They have not comprehended the faculties and fields of sense, so they have false understandings that lead them into deluded states, where they lose the true basis completely.

Concerned only with hurriedly striving for leadership, they are falsely called teachers; while they value an empty reputation in the world, how can they consider the fact that they are bringing ill upon themselves? Not only do they deafen and blind people of later times, but they also cause the current teaching to degenerate. Having climbed to the high and wide seat of a spiritual master, instead they lie on iron bedsteads, suffering the final shame of Chunda [whose offering caused the death of Buddha], forced to drink molten copper.

Beware! It is not good to be complacent with oneself. The punishment consequent on slandering the Great Vehicle is not minor.

2. On Factional Sectarianism and Failure to Penetrate Controversies

The Zen founder did not come from India to China because there is something to be transmitted. He just pointed directly to the human mind for the perception of its essence and realization of awakening. How could there be any sectarian style to be valued?

Nevertheless, the provisional teachings devised by the guides to the source had differences and accordingly came to differ from one another. For example, the two masters Hui-neng and Shen-hsiu had the same teacher, but their perceptions and understandings differed. Hence the world referred to them as the Southern School and the Northern School.

Once Hui-neng was gone, there were two teachers, Hsing-ssu and Huai-jang, who continued his teaching. Hsing-ssu taught Hsi-ch'ien, and Huai-jang taught Ma-tsu. Ma-tsu was also called Chiang-hsi, and Hsi-ch'ien was also called Shih-t'ou.

From these two branches diverged individual lineages, each occupying a region. The outflow of the original streams cannot be recorded in full. When it got to Te-shan, Lin-chi, Kuei-shan and Yang-shan, Ts'ao-shan and Tung-shan, Hsueh-feng, Yun-

men, and so on, each school had established devices, with higher
and lower gradations.

But when it came to continuation, their descendants main-
tained sects and factionalized their ancestries. Not basing themselves on reality, eventually they produced many sidetracks,
contradicting and clashing with one another, so that the profound and the shallow became indistinguishable.

Unfortunately, they still do not realize that the Great Way
takes no sides; streams of truth are all of the same flavor. These
sectarians spread embellishments in empty space and stick nee-
dles in iron and stone, taking disputation for superknowledge
and lip-flapping for meditation. Sword-points of approval and
disapproval arise, and mountains of egotism toward others
stand tall. In their anger they become monsters, their views and
interpretations ultimately turning them into outsiders. Unless
they meet good friends, they will hardly be able to get out of
the harbor of delusion. They bring on bad results, even from
good causes.

3. On Teaching and Preaching Without Knowing the Bloodline

If you want to expound the vehicle to the source and bring
out the essentials of the Teaching, unless you know the blood-
line all you are doing is wrongly propagating heresies.

In this context, there is first extolling and then upholding,
criticizing, or praising doctrines, snapping the thrust of intellect. When one is in charge of carrying out the imperative of
Zen, enlivening and killing are in one's hands.

Sometimes one stands like a mile-high wall, totally inacces-
sible, or sometimes one may consent to let go temporarily and
follow the waves. Like a king wielding a sword, the ideal is to
attain autonomy.

Active function is a matter of appropriate timing; one grants
or deprives like a grand general. Waves leap, peaks tower, light-

ning flashes, and wind rushes; the elephant king strolls, the true lion roars.

We often see those who do not assess their own strength but steal the words of others. They know how to let go but not how to gather in; they may have enlivening, but they have no killing. They do not distinguish servant from master or true from false; they insult the ancients and bury the essence of Zen.

Everyone figures and calculates in their conceptual faculties, speculating and searching within compounded elements of mind and matter. Since they are ignorant of the enlightenment right before their eyes, they attain only imitation insight.

How could it be an easy matter to set up the banner of the teaching on a nonabiding basis, to preach in the place of Buddha? Have you not seen how the great master Yun-men said, "In all of China it is hard to find anyone at all who can bring up a saying"?

And have you not seen how Master Huang-po said, "Grand Master Ma produced over eighty teachers; when questioned, each spoke fluently, but only Master Lu-shan amounts to anything"?

Thus we know that when one takes up this position, if one understands how to give direction and guidance, then one is a complete Zen master. How do we know this? Have you not seen how an ancient said, "Know the soil by the sprouts; know people by what they say"? One is already revealed at once even in blinking the eyes and raising the brows; how much the more in being an examplar. How could one not be careful?

4. On Giving Answers Without Observing Time and Situation and Not Having the Eye of the Source

Anyone who would be a guide to the source first distinguishes the false from the true. Once the false and the true have been distinguished, it is also essential that the time and situation be understood. It is, furthermore, necessary to speak with the eye of the source, able to make a point and to respond without inconsistency.

Thus, although there is nothing personal in a statement, we still make provisional use of discernment of the aim within words. The Ts'ao-Tung has "knocking and calling out" for its function, the Lin-chi has "interchange" for its working; Yun-men "contains, covers, and cuts off the flows"; while the Kuei-Yang silently matches square and round. Like a valley echoing melodies, like matching talismans at a pass, although they are different in their manners, that does not inhibit their fluid integration.

In recent generations, Zen teachers have lost the basis; students have no guidance. They match wits egotistically and take what is ephemeral for an attainment. Where is the heart to guide others? No longer do we hear of knowledge to destroy falsehood. Caning and shouting at random, they say they have studied Te-shan and Lin-chi; presenting circular symbols to each other, they claim they have deeply understood Kuei-shan and Yang-shan.

Since they do not handle the all-embracing source in their answers, how can they know the essential eye in their actions? They fool the young and deceive the sagacious. Truly they bring on the laughter of objective observers and call calamity upon their present state. This is why the Overnight Illuminate said, "If you do not want to incur hellish karma, do not slander the Buddha's true teaching."

People like this cannot be all told of. They just leave their teachers' heritage without any insight of their own. Having no basis upon which to rely, their restless consciousness is unclear. They are only to be pitied, but it is hard to inform them of this.

5. On Discrepancy between Principle and Fact, and Failure to Distinguish Defilement and Purity

The schools of the enlightened ones always include both principle and fact. Facts are established on the basis of principle, while principle is revealed by means of facts. Principles and facts complement one another like eyes and feet. If you have facts without principle, you get stuck in the mud and cannot get through; if you have principle without facts, you will be vague and without resort. If you want them to be nondual, it is best that they be completely merged.

Take the example of the manner of the House of Ts'ao-Tung: they have the relative and absolute, light and darkness. The Lin-chi have host and guest, substance and function. Although their provisional teachings are not the same, their bloodlines commune. There is not one that does not include the others; when mobilized, all are mustered. It is also like *Contemplation of the Realm of Reality*, which discusses both noumenal principle and phenomenal fact, refuting both inherent solidity and voidness.

The nature of the ocean is boundless, yet it is contained in the tip of a hair; the polar mountain is enormous, yet it can be hidden in a seed. Surely it is not the perception of saints that makes it thus; the design of reality is just so. It is not miraculous display of supernatural powers, either, or forced appellations of something false by nature. It is not to be sought from another; it all comes from mind's creation.

Buddhas and sentient beings are equal, so if you do not realize this truth, there will be idle discussion, causing the defiled and the pure to be indistinct and the true and the false to be undifferentiated. Relative and absolute get stuck in interchange; substance and function are mixed up in spontaneity. This is described in these terms: "If a single thing is not clear, fine dust covers the eyes." If one cannot eliminate one's own illness, how can one cure the diseases of others? You should be most careful and thoroughgoing; it is certainly not a trivial matter.

6. On Subjective Judgment of Ancient and Contemporary Sayings Without Going Through Clarification

Once people have joined an association for intensive study, they must select a teacher and then associate with good companions. A teacher is needed to point out the road; companions are valuable for refinement. If you only want self-understanding, then how can you lead on younger students and bring out the teaching of the school? Where is the will to deal with people to their benefit?

Observe how the worthies of the past traversed mountains and seas, not shrinking from death or life, for the sake of one or two sayings. When there was the slightest tinge of doubt, the matter had to be submitted to certain discernment; what they wanted was distinct clarity. First becoming standards of truth versus falsehood, acting as eyes for humanity and the angels, only after that did they raise the seal of the school on high and circulate the true teaching, bringing out the rights and wrongs of former generations, bearing down on inconclusive cases.

If you make your own subjective judgment of past and present without having undergone purification and clarification, how is that different from performing a sword dance without having learned how to handle a sword, or foolishly counting on getting across a pit without having sized it up? Can you avoid cutting your hand or falling?

One who chooses well is like a king goose picking out milk from water; one who chooses poorly is like a sacred tortoise leaving tracks. Especially in this context, where there is negative and positive activity and expression of mutual interchange, to come to life in a way that turns morbid is to relegate the absolute to the relative. It is not right to give rein to the unruly mind and use it as it is to try to fathom the meaning of the sages. This is especially true in view of the fact that the essence of the one-word teaching has myriad methods of setting up teachings. Can we not be careful of this, to prevent opposition?

7. On Memorizing Slogans Without Being Capable of Subtle Function Meeting the Needs of the Time

It is not that there is no guidance for students of transcendent insight, but once you have gotten guidance, it is essential that expanded function actually appear; only then do you have a little bit of intimate realization. If you just stick to a school and memorize slogans, it is not penetrating enlightenment at all, but mere intellectual knowledge.

This is why the ancients said, "When your view equals your teacher, you have less than half your teacher's virtue. Only when your view is beyond your teacher can you bring out the teacher's teaching." The Sixth Patriarch, furthermore, said to Elder Ming, "What I have told you is not something secret; the secret is within you." And Yen-t'ou said to Hsueh-feng, "Everything flows forth from your own heart."

So we know that speaking, caning, and hollering do not depend on a teacher's bequest; how could the marvelous function, free in all ways, demand another's assent?

When you degrade them, pearls and gold lose their beauty; when you prize them, shards and pebbles shine. If you go when and as you should go, principle and fact are both mastered; if you act when and as you should act, there is not the slightest miss.

The stuff of a real man is not for sissies. Don't be a servile literalist and get stuck on verbal expressions as if this were the manner of Zen, or flap your lips and beat your gums as if this were sublime understanding. This cannot be penetrated by language or known by thought. Wisdom comes out in the village

of infinite nothingness; spirituality is found in the realm of un-
fathomability. Where dragons and elephants tread is not within
the capability of asses.

8. On Failure to Master the Scriptures and Adducing Proofs Wrongly

Whoever would bring out the vehicle of Zen and cite the doctrines of the Teaching must first understand what the Buddha
meant, then accord with the mind of Zen masters. Only after
that can you bring them up and put them into practice, compar-
ing degrees of closeness.

If, in contrast, you do not know the doctrines and principles
but just stick to a sectarian methodology, when you adduce
proofs readily but wrongly, you will bring slander and criticism
on yourself.

Yet the canon of sutras is nothing but pointing out tracks; the
complete all-at-once Higher Vehicle is just like a signpost. Even
if you can understand a hundred thousand concentrations and
countless doctrines and methods, you only increase your own
toil and do not get at the issue.

What is more, comprehending the provisional and returning
to the absolute, gathering the outgrowths back to the source,
not admitting a single atom in the realm of absolute purity while
not rejecting anything in the methodology of enlightened activity, inevitably deciding the case on the basis of the facts, getting
to the substance and removing the complications, has no connection whatsoever with the source of Zen.

There are many great people who are experts in the scriptures, real devotees of broad knowledge of the ancients, who
flaunt their eloquence like sharp blades and set forth their
wealth of learning like stocks in a storehouse; when they get
here, they must be taught to be still and silent, so that the road
of speech cannot be extended. Finding that all their memoriza-

tion of words and phrases has been an account of others' treasures, for the first time they will believe in the specialty of Zen, which is the separate transmission outside of doctrine.

Younger people should not bog themselves down, incurring the derision of others and disgracing the way of Zen. Do not say you do not need cultivation, or consider a little bit enough. Since you do not even understand the outgrowths, how can you realize the root?

9. On Indulging in Making Up Songs and Verses Without Regard for Meter and Without Having Arrived at Reality

There are many styles of song and verse in Zen; some are short, some long, some modern, some ancient. They use sound and form to reveal practical application, or call on events to express states. Some follow principle to talk of reality; some oppose the trend of affairs to rectify customs and morals.

Thus, although their approaches are different—which is inevitable, since their inspirations were different—they all bring out the great cause. Together they extol the meditations of the Buddha, inspiring students of later times and criticizing the intelligent people of former times. In each case, the main meaning is in the words, so how could it be proper to compose them arbitrarily?

Sometimes I see established Zen teachers and advanced students of meditation who consider songs and verses to be leisure pursuits and consider composition to be a trivial matter. They spit out whatever they feel, and in many cases their works are similar to vulgar sayings. Composed on impulse, they are just like common talk.

These people say of themselves that they are not concerned by coarseness and are not picky about grubbiness; they are thus trying to suggest that theirs are words beyond worldly convention, advertising them as hearkening back to ultimate truth. The knowledgeable laugh in derision when they read them, while fools believe in them and circulate them. They cause the principles of names to gradually disappear, and add to the growing weakness of the doctrinal schools.

Have you not seen the tens of thousands of verses of the *Flower Ornament Scripture* and the thousands of poems of the Zen masters? Both are profuse and vivid, with elegant language; all of them are refined and pure, without padding. They are hardly the same as imitation of worldly customs with all their fripperies.

For writing to be a pathway in later times and true in the mouths of the multitudes, it is still necessary to study precedents, and then it is essential to suit it to the occasion. If you happen to have little natural ability, then you should be natural and content with simplicity; why pretend to genius or aspire to intellectual brilliance?

If you spout vulgar inanities, you disturb the influence of the Way. Weaving miserable misconceptions, you cause trouble. Unconvincing falsehoods will increase later disgrace.

10. On Defending One's Own Shortcomings and Indulging in Contention

As the land is full of religious communes and the Zen societies are extremely numerous, with communities numbering not less than half a thousand gathered there, are there not one or two working for the furtherance of the Teaching?

There are some people among them who embrace the Way, people of pure conduct, who agree to temporarily go along with the feelings of the community and exert their strength to continue the Zen teaching, gather colleagues from all over, and establish a site of enlightenment in one region. With morning questioning and even assembly, they do not shy away from toil and hardship, wanting only to continue the life of wisdom of the buddhas, guiding beginners.

They do not do it for the sake of increasing fame or out of greed for profit and support; rather, like a bell ringing when struck, they dispense medicine when they encounter illness. Showering the rain of the Teaching, they have no bias toward great or small; as they sound the thunder of the Teaching, far and near all respond. Their prosperity or austerity naturally varies, their activity and concealment differ; but this is not on account of choosiness or because of attachment and rejection.

There are those who inherit succession by sycophancy, who hold position by stealing rank and then claim to have attained the highest vehicle and to have transcended mundane things. They defend their own shortcomings and derogate the strengths of others. Fooling around in cocoons of ignorance, they smack their lips in front of meat markets. Emphasizing their temporal power, they take pride in glibness.

They gossip and call that compassion; they are sloppy and call that virtue in action. Violating Buddhist prohibitions and precepts, abandoning the dignity of the religious community, they disparage the Two Vehicles and wrongly dispense with the three studies. What is more, they fail to investigate the great matter, yet approve of themselves as masters.

Thus, at the end of the age of imitation, the demons are strong and the Teaching is weak. They use the Buddha's robe of righteousness to steal the benevolence and dignity of kings. Their mouths speak of the basis of liberation, but their minds play with the obsessions of ghosts and spirits. Since they have no shame or conscience, how can they avoid wrongdoing?

Now I have exposed these folks to warn people in the future. Meeting with a chance for wisdom is not a small matter; choosing a teacher is most difficult. If you can bear the responsibility yourself, eventually you will fulfill maximum potential. I am forcibly dispensing a stunning medicine, willing to be subjected to slander and hatred, so that people on the same path may be assisted in awakening.

YUNG-MING

False Cults

BECAUSE OF IGNORANCE of the qualites of inherent nature, people fail to understand the true source. Abandoning enlightenment, they follow the dusts, giving up the root for the branches. They get hung up in the demonic web of being and nonbeing, and they wander in the forest of errors of oneness and difference. Trying to master true emptiness, they become alienated from the nature of reality; based on the arising and disappearance of sense data, they follow the being and nothingness of objects. Clinging to nihilism, confused by eternalism, they pursue the conditional and forget the essential. Mistakenly developing intellectual interpretation, they cultivate practice wrongly.

Some mellow the spirit, nurture energy, and preserve naturalness. Some torture the body, mortifying the flesh, and consider that the ultimate path.

Some cling to nongrasping and stand rooted in the immediate environment. Some suppress the wandering mind in quest of quiet meditation.

Some get rid of feelings and negate phenomena in order to stabilize voidness. Some stick to reflections, get involved in objects, and embrace forms.

Some extinguish the true radiance of the spiritual source. Some eliminate the true causal basis of Buddhist principles.

Some cut off consciousness and freeze the mind, experiencing an inanimate state in consequence. Some clear the mind and ignore matter, abiding as a result in a kind of celestial state in which it is hard to become enlightened.

Some stick to phantasms, clinging to their existence. Some become complete nihilists.

Some eliminate all views and dwell in dark rooms. Some insist on perception and dwell on cognition.

Some consider having awareness to be the form of the true Buddha. Some imitate insentience, like wood or stone.

Some cling to illusion as if it were the same as the ultimate realization, like considering clay in itself to be a jar. Some seek ways of liberation wrongly focused, like seeking water while rejecting waves.

Some hasten outwardly and deludedly produce dream states. Some keep to inwardness and live in solemnity, embracing ignorance.

Some are devoted to oneness and consider everything the same. Some see differences and define individual reality-realms.

Some keep to ignorant nondiscrimination and consider that the Great Way. Some value the notion of voidness and consider denial of good and bad to be true practice.

Some interpret inconceivability to be insensate voidness. Some understand true goodness and subtle form to be really existent.

Some stop mental workings and cut off thoughts, like angels with polluted minds. Some contemplate with awareness and attention, falling within the bounds of intellectual assessment.

Some fail to investigate the nature of illusion thoroughly, interpreting it as the unknown beginning. Some are ignorant of illusory substance and make a religion of nothingness.

Some recognize reflections as realities. Some seek reality while clinging to falsehood.

Some recognize the nature of perception as a living thing. Some point to illusory objects as inanimate.

Some willfully entertain ideas and turn away from silent knowledge. Some cut off thoughts and thus lack enlightened function.

Some lose sight of natural qualities and conceive views of matter and mind. Some rely on ultimate emptiness and develop a nihilistic attitude.

Some cling to universal principle and immediately abandon adornment. Some misunderstand gradual teaching and become fanatical activists.

Some detach from objects by relying on essence but make their attachment to self stronger. Some ignore everything and maintain themselves in ignorance.

Some decide that persons and phenomena are as they are naturally, and fall into the idea that there is no causality. Some cling to the combination of objects and intellect and conceive the notion of collective causality.

Some cling to the mixing of mind and objects, confusing subjective and objective actualities. Some stick to distinguishing absolute and conventional, bound up in the folly of obstruction by knowledge.

Some adhere to unchanging oneness, thus falling into eternalism. Some determine the movement of origin, abiding, decay, and nothingness, thus sinking into nihilism.

Some cling to noncultivation and thus dismiss the ranks of sages. Some say there is realization, and thus turn away from natural reality.

Some delight in the environment and their own persons, thus following the routines of the world. Some reject life and death and thus lose true liberation.

Some, misunderstanding true emptiness, are devoted to causes and obsessed with results. Some, ignorant of ultimate reality, long for enlightenment and despise bewilderment.

Some cling to expedient statements, holding to them as literal truth. Some lose the reality of verbal expression and seek silence apart from words.

Some are devoted to doctrinal methods and disdain spontaneous meditation. Some promote meditative contemplations and repudiate the measuring devices of the complete teaching.

Some compete at being extraordinary while only being concerned with status, suddenly sinking in the sea of knowledge. Some contrive purity to find out hidden secrets, instead getting trapped within a realm of shadows.

Some produce extraordinary intellectual interpretations, gouging flesh and producing wounds. Some dwell on original essential purity but cling to the medicine so it becomes unhealthy.

Some pursue the literature, searching out meanings, and wind up drinking a flood. Some keep to stillness and live in isolation, sitting in the dust of dogma.

Some discuss the formless Great Vehicle with the idea of getting something. Some search for mystic truth outside of things by means of calculating thoughts.

Some reject explanation and conceive the notion of absolute nonverbalization. Some keep explanation and call on the criticism of clinging to the pointing finger.

Some approve of active function and remain at the root source of birth and death. Some concentrate on memorization, dwelling within the limits of conscious thinking.

Some lose the essence of complete awareness by modification and adjustment. Some let be whatever will be, and lack a method of entering the path.

Some initiate energetic physical and mental efforts and linger in contrivance. Some keep to letting be without concern and sink into the bondage of insight.

Some concentrate on focusing thoughts and contemplating diligently, thus losing correct reception. Some imitate uninhibited freedom and give up cultivation.

Some follow binding compulsions while presuming upon intrinsic emptiness. Some cling to bondage and try to eliminate it arbitrarily.

Some are so serious that they develop attachment to religion. Some are so flippant that they ruin the basis of enlightenment.

Some seek so aggressively that they turn away from the original mind. Some slack off and become heedless.

Some lack realism, their speech and their realization differing. Some violate the vehicle of enlightenment by disparity of being and action.

Some keep to tranquillity, dwelling in emptiness, thereby losing the nature of great compassion. Some ignore conditions and reject the temporal, thus missing the door of naturalness.

Some stick to the notion of self, thus being ignorant of the emptiness of person. Some confuse immediate experience and harden their attachment to doctrine.

Some interpret without having faith, increasing false views. Some have faith but no understanding, increasing ignorance.

Some affirm the subjective but deny the objective. Some claim states are deep while knowledge is shallow.

Some get confused about the nature of things by grasping. Some turn away from immediate reality by rejection.

Some violate cause because of detachment. Some forget consequences because of attachment.

Some repudiate reality by denial. Some ruin temporary expedients by affirmation.

Some hate ignorance but thereby turn their backs on the door of immutable knowledge. Some dislike varying states but thereby destroy absorption in the nature of reality.

Some base themselves on the principle of sameness but thereby develop conceit. Some dismiss differentiations, thus destroying the methods of expedient techniques.

Some affirm enlightenment but repudiate the cycle of true teaching. Some deny sentient beings and repudiate the true body of Buddha.

Some stick to basic knowledge and deny expedient wisdom. Some miss the true source and cling to temporary methods.

Some linger in noumenon, sinking into a pit of inaction. Some cling to phenomena, throwing themselves into the net of illusion.

Some annihilate boundaries and obliterate tracks, turning away from the door of dual illumination. Some maintain rectitude, keeping to the center, but lose the sense of expedient technique.

Some cultivate concentration or insight one-sidedly, without balance, thus rotting the sprouts of the path. Some carry out vows all alone, burying the family of the enlightened.

Some work on the practice of inaction to cultivate fabricated enlightenment. Some cling to the nonclinging mind, learning imitation insight.

Some aim for purity, misunderstanding the true nature of defilement. Some dwell on the absolute and lose the basic emptiness of the mundane.

Some practice formless contemplation, blocking true suchness. Some conceive a sense of knowing but thereby turn away from the essence of reality.

Some stick by true explanation but develop literalistic views. Some drink the elixir of immortality yet die young.

Some are so earnest about the principle of completeness that they develop an attitude of clinging attachment; they drink the nectar but turn it into poison.

The foregoing has been a brief notice of one hundred twenty kinds of views and understandings characteristic of false cults. All of them have lost the source and turned away from the essential message.

The Cooperation of Concentration and Insight

In Zen and the Teachings there are two methods, most honored of the myriad practices of ten perfections. At first they are called stopping and seeing, to help new learners; later they become concentration and wisdom, roots of enlightenment.

These are only one reality, which seems to have two parts. In the silence of the essence of reality is stopping by comprehending truth; when silent yet ever aware, subtle seeing is there.

Concentration is the father, insight the mother; they can conceive the thousand sages, developing their faculties and powers, nurturing their sacred potential, giving birth to buddhas and Zen masters in every moment of thought.

Concentration is the general, insight the minister; they can assist the mind monarch in attaining the unexcelled, providing forever means for all to realize the Way, in the manner of the enlightenment of the ancient buddhas.

Concentration is like the moonlight shining so brightly that the stars of errant falsehood vanish. If you can hold up the torch of knowledge, so much the clearer. Irrigating the sprouts of enlightenment, it removes emotional bondage.

Insight is like the sun shining, breaking up the darkness of ignorance. It is able to cause the Zen of the ignorant with false views to turn into transcendent wisdom.

A brief time of silence, a moment of stillness, gradually build up into correct concentration. The sages, making comparatively little effort, ultimately saw the subtle essence of the pedestal of the spirit.

As soon as you hear even a little bit of the Teaching, it can influence your subconscious such that seeds of awakening develop. The moment you turn the light of awareness around, accurate cognition opens up; in an instant you can accomplish Buddha's teaching like this.

The power of meditative concentration is inconceivable; it changes the ordinary into sages instantly. Boundless birth and death is thereby severed at the root; the nest of accumulated ages of mundane toils is destroyed. This is the water that stills the mind, the pearl that purifies the will; its light engulfs myriad forms, lighting a thousand roads.

When you open your own eyes, there are no obstructions; originally there is nothing in the world that constrains. When thieves of attention and reflection are quelled in a timely manner, then the sickness of obsession with objects suddenly clears up.

Washing away the dirt of thoughts and cleaning away the dust of confusion reveals the body of reality and strengthens the life of wisdom. Like an immutable mountain, like a still sea, even if the sky should flip and the earth overturn, you would not be changed. Bright as crystal imbued with moonlight, serene and unbound, you are independent.

No one can measure the insight of wisdom; it naturally manifests the light of the mind according to the occasion. It is the leader of myriad practices, the spiritual ruler at all times. It evaporates the ocean of misery and shatters the mountains of falsehood.

When the clouds of illusion withdraw completely for a while, the gold in the poor woman's house shows up all at once, and the pearl embedded in the wrestler's forehead re-emerges. Cutting through the web of folly, interrupting the flow of desires, the awesome power of the great hero has no peer; it can cool the iron beds and copper stakes of hell and cause the results of the actions of demons and antagonists to cease. Settling disputes, fulfilling honor and justice, everywhere it shows people the wisdom of the buddhas. Biased and perverted knowledge is all subordinated to the source; both the smallest and the greatest alike receive direction.

One-sided cultivation of concentration is pure yin; it corrodes people and erodes right livelihood. If you use accurate insight to illuminate meditation, all things will naturally be clear as a mirror.

One-sided cultivation of insight is pure yang; it withers people and makes them linger on the way. You should use subtle concentration to help contemplative exercise, like the clear light of the moon removing a film of mist.

I recommend equal cultivation of concentration and insight, not one-sided practice. They are originally one entity, not two things. It is like a bird flying through the sky with two wings, or like a chariot drawn on two wheels. Thus in the course of ordinary life you climb up onto the shore of awakening, then sail the boat of compassion on the ocean of karma.

There is concentration on the concrete, in which everything is accomplished by placing the mind on one point. There is concentration on the abstract, in which one must only look directly into the essential nature of mind.

There is contemplation of the concrete, in which one clarifies the characteristics of things and develops judgment. There is contemplation of the abstract, in which it is suddenly realized there is no One and no Beyond.

Insofar as concentration itself is insight, they are not one, not two, not any calculation of mind. Insofar as insight itself is concentration, they are not the same, not different, beyond looking and listening.

Sometimes they are operated together, so you are tranquil yet perceptive, penetrating the teaching of the real. Sometimes they both disappear; neither concentration nor insight, this transcends ordinary standards.

Entering concentration in one atom and arising from it in a multitude of atoms is something natural in the context of transcendent insight. While absorbed in the state of a child, you discuss the laws of reality in the state of an elderly person. If you can see into a single object, all objects are the same; an atom near at hand or a land far away—all are comprehended. On the road of true suchness, you discourse on birth and death; in the ocean of ignorance, you expound the complete religion. The eye can do the enlightened work of the nose; entering concentration in an atom of matter, you arise from concentration in an atom of scent.

Mind and objects are always the same; it is views that differ. Who speaks of not working on cultivation—waves are originally water. Neither silent nor shining, beyond words and thought, yet tranquil and perceptive, effective without compare: temporal and true both carried out, you open the right road; substance and function helping each other, you embody the subtle message.

I urge you not to throw away time, for it's swift as an arrow, fast as a stream. Distraction is entirely due to lack of concentration; stupidity and blindness are caused by lack of true knowledge.

Genuinely true words should be admitted into the ears. A thousand scriptures and ten thousand treatises indicate the same thing: the total effect of concentration and insight should never be forgotten—in a single moment you return at once to the state of real awakeness.

Concentration needs practice; insight needs learning. Don't let the spiritual pedestal be dimmed at all.

A massive tree grows from a tiny sprout; effective work gradually accumulated produces value and excellence. Even an ape that learns concentration is born in a heavenly realm; a little girl, with a moment's thought, enters the door of the Way.

When you can help yourself and also help others, then cause and effect are fulfilled; no one can talk of doing this without concentration and insight.

Glossary of Proper Names, Technical Terms, and Zen Stories

Sanskrit Names

ANANDA   One of Buddha's major disciples, particularly noted for learning. See *Transmission of Light*, chapter 3.

ARYADEVA   Reckoned as the fifteenth Indian patriarch of Zen, Aryadeva (also called Kanadeva) was a disciple of the great Buddhist philosopher Nagarjuna and also a distinguished metaphysician himself. See *Transmission of Light*, chapter 16.

AVALOKITESHVARA   A prototypical bodhisattva, or enlightening being. The name literally means "the capacity of objective observation." This figure represents compassion. See *The Flower Ornament Scripture*, pages 1275–1279.

BRAHMA   A Hindu god, especially associated with creation.

DIPANKARA BUDDHA   Also referred to in Chinese by a translation of the name, "Lamp," Dipankara was, according to illustrative tradition, a buddha of high antiquity in whose presence Shakyamuni Buddha was originally inspired to seek buddhahood.

INDRA   "King of gods," Indra is a Hindu deity presiding over thirty-three celestial domains.

MAHASTHAMAPRAPTA   A prototypical bodhisattva, representing spiritual power, popular in Pure Land Buddhist tradition. The name means "Imbued with Great Power."

MANJUSHRI   A prototypical bodhisattva, representing wisdom and knowledge. The name means "Glorious One." See *The Flower Ornament Scripture*, books 9 and 10.

NAGARJUNA   Sometimes considered the greatest Buddhist thinker after Buddha himself, Nagarjuna is the author of the seminal work on emptiness and the Middle Way. He is also traditionally said to have been responsible for recovering the *Prajnaparamita* and *Avatamsaka* scriptures from another realm of consciousness. Nagarjuna is traditionally considered the fourteenth Indian patriarch of Zen and also a patriarch or "patron saint" of T'ien-t'ai, Pure Land, and Tantric Buddhism. See *Transmission of Light*, chapter 15.

SAMANTABHADRA   A prototypical bodhisattva, "Universal Good," representing practical commitment and action. Also represents the totality of the bodhisattva work. See *The Flower Ornament Scripture*, pages 176–181 and 1503–1518.

SHAKYAMUNI   This name refers to Gautama, the historical Buddha.

TATHAGATA   An epithet of buddhas, meaning those who have arrived at suchness, or objective reality.

VAIROCHANA   The primordial "Cosmic Sun Buddha," Vairochana represents pure awareness or the "body of light."

VIMALAKIRTI   A scriptural figure, a completely enlightened buddha who is also a householder. Vimalakirti, whose name means "Pure Name" or "Undefiled Repute," stands for the Dharma itself. See *The Blue Cliff Record*, story 84.

YAJNADATTA   This name refers to an illustrative story commonly used in Zen. A man named Yajnadatta looked in the mirror one day and didn't see his face. Not realizing the mirror had been reversed and he was looking at the unreflective back side, Yajnadatta rushed around in a frenzy, thinking he had lost his head. This represents the way we tend to get lost in objects and influenced by situations and so forget our real minds and real selves.

Chinese Names

GRAND MASTER MA   Ma Tsu, a brilliant eighth-century master, disciple of Huai-jang (q.v.) and teacher of most of the Zen masters of the generation succeeding him. Ma Tsu and Hsi-ch'ien (Shih-t'ou) were considered the greatest teachers of their time, and many of their students studied with both of them.

HSI-CH'IEN   More commonly referred to as Shih-t'ou. An outstanding master of the eighth century, author of the early classic *Ts'an T'ung Ch'i,* or "Integration of Differentiation and Unity."

HSING-SSU   An eighth-century master, disciple of Hui-neng, the Sixth Patriarch of Zen according to the reckoning of the Southern School. Hsing-ssu was the teacher of Shih-t'ou and is regarded as the common ancestor of the Zen Houses of Ts'ao-Tung, Yun-men, and Fa-yen.

HUAI-JANG   An eighth-century master, disciple of Hui-neng, the Sixth Patriarch of Zen. Huai-jang was the teacher of Ma Tsu and is regarded as the common ancestor of the Zen Houses of Kuei-Yang and Lin-chi.

HUI-NENG   The Sixth Patriarch or Grand Master of Zen, according to the reckoning of the Southern School of Zen, which followed him and ultimately grew to overwhelming predominance over other schools of Zen, such as the Northern School and the Ox Head School. According to tradition, Hui-neng, who died in the early eighth century, was an illiterate woodcutter who attained the highest degrees of enlightenment spontaneously, through "the knowledge that has no teacher."

LI T'UNG-HSUAN   An eighth-century lay Buddhist expert on the *Avatamsaka* or *Hua-yen* scripture, author of one of the most famous commentaries. See *The Flower Ornament Scripture,* appendix 3.

LU-SHAN   Zen master Pao-yun, a successor of the eighth-century great Ma Tsu.

MA TSU   See Grand Master Ma.

MASTER CHIH   Pao Chih, an uncanny fifth- to sixth-century mystic, author of didactic poetry prized by Zen Buddhists; also figures in didactic stories.

SENG CHAO   A fourth- or fifth-century Buddhist scholar and mystic, disciple of the famous translator Kumarajiva, author of a number of unusual essays highly esteemed by Zen students.

SHEN-HSIU   A seventh-century Zen master, considered the sixth patriarch of Zen according to the Northern Tradition.

SHIH-T'OU   See Hsi-ch'ien.

SIXTH PATRIARCH   Refers to the Southern Tradition: see Hui-neng.

TE-SHAN   A ninth-century Zen master, teacher of the great Hsueh-feng, ancestor of the Yun-men House of Zen. In Zen lore, Te-shan is represented as occasionally hitting seekers in order to jar them out of closed-circuit thought habits.

YEN-T'OU   An unusual ninth- to tenth-century master, conventionally referred to as a successor of Te-shan; inspired the final enlightenment of Hsueh-feng.

Technical Terms

AGE OF IMITATION   According to Buddhist tradition, the teaching goes through three general periods: true, imitation, and degenerate. There are different reckonings of historical epicycles of the teaching; the one that places the classical Zen masters of China at the end of the age of imitation figures the true teaching to last five hundred years, followed by a thousand years of imitation teaching.

BODHISATTVAS   Enlightening beings; may refer to people who are dedicated to universal enlightenment, or to supernal beings reflecting the essential principles of Buddhism.

CLUSTERS OF MENTAL AND PHYSICAL ELEMENTS   Form, sensation, perception, conditioning, and consciousness.

COMPLETE ALL-AT-ONCE   The most advanced mode of teaching and learning, according to the T'ien-t'ai school of Buddhism, in which the totality of truth is represented as a whole and apprehended in a nonsequential mode.

CONCENTRATION AND WISDOM   Essential ingredients of Zen meditation. Without wisdom, concentration exaggerates and perpetuates flaws of character; without concentration, wisdom is unstable and hard to apply.

CONTEMPLATION OF THE REALM OF REALITY   A seminal contemplation guide by Tu Shun (557–640), considered the founder of the Hua-yen or Flower Ornament school of Buddhism in China, based on the scripture by that name. Tu Shun's work was also valued by Zen Buddhists. The work in question, with a detailed explanation by a later master, is translated in full in my *Entry into the Inconceivable: An Introduction to Hua-Yen Buddhism* (University of Hawaii Press, 1983).

EIGHT CONCENTRATIONS   A system of meditation consisting of the four stages of meditation (q.v.) plus the four formless attainments of absorption in infinity of space, absorption in infinity of consciousness, absorption in infinity of nothingness, and absorption in neither perception nor nonperception.

EIGHT TEACHINGS   A classification scheme of T'ien-t'ai Buddhism for encompassing the diverse totality of Buddhist teachings within a single framework. The Eight Teachings refer to four levels of doctrine and four modes of teaching. The four levels of doctrine are called Tripitaka, referring to the elementary teachings; Common, referring to the teaching of emptiness common to all bodhisattvas; Separate, referring to unitarian teachings perceptible only to higher bodhisattvas; and Complete, for the highest bodhisattvas, in which the totality of truth is reflected all at once. The four modes are gradual, sudden, unfixed, and secret.

FACE A WALL   This represents ignorance and inability to cope with differentiation.

FIRE HEXAGRAM   A symbolic figure from the ancient Chinese *I Ching*. The Fire trigram consists of two solid lines with a broken line between them; the Fire hexagram consists of two Fire trigrams, one on top of the other. In Zen usage, this figure symbolizes integration of the relative and the absolute, and integration of the discursive and intuitive modes of cognition through which the relative and absolute are discerned.

FIVE TIMES   A T'ien-t'ai Buddhist classification scheme, designed to group scriptures categorically according to a particular type of teaching proper to a particular time envisioned in the teaching career of Buddha. The first time is that of the *Flower Ornament Scripture*, when Buddha first revealed his whole enlightenment after his awakening. The second time is called that of the shallows, when Buddha backtracked to teach elementary methods of self-purification, in view of the inability of the vast majority to understand the *Flower Ornament* at first. The third time is called that of rebuke, or turning from the small to the great. This is when attachment to elementary methodology is rebuked and the perspective of Mahayana Buddhism is introduced. The fourth time is that of the perfection of wisdom, in which all attachments are resolved in emptiness. The fifth is the time of the Lotus and Great Demise, in which Buddha preached the unity and eternity of truth and the universality of the essence of buddhahood.

FIVE VEHICLES   Variously defined in T'ien-t'ai and Hua-yen Buddhism, these represent different levels of aspiration and action, ranging from social morality, enhancement of consciousness, and inner peace to higher enlightenment and complete awakening of mind.

FOUR STAGES OF MEDITATION   The first stage is defined by attention, reflection, joy, bliss, and single-mindedness. The second stage is defined by inner purity, joy, bliss, and single-mindedness. The third stage is defined by equanimity, recollection, insight, bliss, and single-mindedness. The fourth stage is defined by neither pain nor pleasure, equanimity, recollection, and single-mindedness.

GHEE A symbol of buddha nature, which is considered a latent potential within the human mind, just as ghee (clarified butter) is a latent potential in milk.

LAMP BUDDHA Dipankara Buddha (q.v.); symbolizes primordial awareness.

MOUNT HENG One of the five sacred mountains of China.

ONE VEHICLE Sanskrit *Ekayana*; this term refers to the most comprehensive manifestations of Buddhism. The One Vehicle is perceived, understood, and defined in different ways. Of particular interest is the complementary contrast between the "centripetal" unitarianism of the *Saddharmapundarika-sutra*, or Lotus scripture, and the "centrifugal" unitarianism of the *Avatamsaka-sutra*, or Flower Ornament scripture. The *Sandhinirmocana-sutra*, which gives the philosophy and technology of Buddhist yoga, expounds the Ekayana concept in terms of the unity of absolute truth. The unitarianism of Zen is rooted in what is called One Mind, or a unified mind, from which perspective it is able to accommodate both Lotus and Flower Ornament visions of unity as well as the unity of absolute truth.

SIX COURSES OF MUNDANE EXISTENCE Animals (symbolizing folly), ghosts (symbolizing greed), titans (symbolizing aggression), hells (symbolizing folly, greed, and hatred together), humanity (symbolizing social virtues), and heavens (symbolizing meditation states).

SIX PERFECTIONS Generosity, morality, tolerance, diligence, meditation, and insight.

STOPPING AND SEEING The two sides of meditation; stopping delusion and seeing truth.

TATHAGATA An epithet of buddhas.

TEN ABODES Initial determination; preparing the ground; practical action; noble birth; fulfillment of skill in means; correct state of mind; nonregression; youthful nature; prince of the teaching; and coronation. See *The Flower Ornament Scripture*, book 15.

TEN DEDICATIONS   Dedication to saving all sentient beings without having any mental image of sentient beings; indestructible dedication; dedication equal to all buddhas; dedication reaching all places; dedication of inexhaustible treasuries of virtue; dedication causing all roots of goodness to endure; dedication equally adapting to all sentient beings; dedication with the character of true thusness; unattached, unbound, liberated dedication; and boundless dedication equal to the cosmos. See *The Flower Ornament Scripture*, book 25.

TEN FAITHS   Elements of mental preparation: faith, mindfulness, diligence, intelligence, concentration, perseverance, stability, dedication, discipline, and commitment.

TEN GREAT DISCIPLES OF BUDDHA   A group of Buddha's disciples, including often-mentioned names like Shariputra, Kasyapa, Subhuti, Ananda, Maudgalyayana, and so on, representing a variety of personalities and psychological types of students.

TEN PERFECTIONS   The six perfections (q.v.), plus vowing, skill in means, power, and knowledge.

TEN PRACTICES   Giving joy; beneficial action; nonopposition; indomitability; nonconfusion; good manifestation; nonattachment; overcoming difficulty; good teaching; and truth. See *The Flower Ornament Scripture*, book 21.

TENTH STAGE   The highest stage of bodhisattvahood. See *The Flower Ornament Scripture*, pages 789–799.

THREE BASKETS   A term for the Buddhist canon.

THREE REALMS OF EXISTENCE   The realm of desire, the realm of form, and the formless realm.

THREE STUDIES   The overall Buddhist curriculum: studies in discipline, concentration, and wisdom.

THREE VEHICLES   Followers, Self-Enlightened, and Bodhisattva; the first two are called lesser; the third is called greater. The first two culminate in individual liberation, and the third is dedicated to universal enlightenment.

THUNDERBOLT IMPLEMENT   A ritual implement used in Tantric Buddhism; in Ts'ao-Tung Zen, it stands for "five in one," referring to the five ranks of Zen as five facets of one reality.

TRIPLEX WORLD   The conditioned world, called triplex in reference to the three realms of desire, form, and formlessness.

TWENTY-FIVE DOMAINS OF BEING   A representation of the spectrum of conditioned mentalities or psychological states.

TWO LESSER VEHICLES   The courses of followers and self-enlightened individuals, whose goal is personal salvation; also called simply "two vehicles."

TWO TRUTHS   Relative truth and absolute truth; all Buddha's teachings are based on the assumption of two truths, often shifting point of reference from relative to absolute and absolute to relative.

UNITARY VEHICLE   See One Vehicle.

WHITE OX ON OPEN GROUND   A symbol of buddha nature revealed.

WRESTLER WITH A GEM EMBEDDED IN HIS FOREHEAD   A symbol of buddha nature concealed.

Zen Stories

MASTER AN'S SAYING ON THE TEACHING HALL   A monk entered the teaching hall of Master Ta-An, looked around, and said, "A fine teaching hall, but there's no one here." The master came through the door and said, "How so?" The monk had no reply.

PAI-CHANG'S SAYING "WHAT IS IT?"   Master Pai-chang drove everyone from his teaching hall, then just as they were leaving, he called to them and said, "What is it?"

TUNG-SHAN'S REPLY TO YUN-YEN'S GINGER-DIGGING SAYING   As Tung-shan was hoeing a ginger plot with Yun-yen, the latter made reference to a Zen master of the past. Tung-shan asked, "Where has this man gone?" Yun-yen remained silent for a good while, then said, "What? What?" Tung-shan said, "Too late!"

Wen-shu and tea drinking   As Wen-shu was drinking tea with
Wu-cho, he held up a crystal cup and asked Wu-cho, "Do they also
have *this* in the South?" Wu-cho replied, "No." Wen-shu said,
"Then what do they usually use for drinking tea?" Wu-cho had no
reply. Later Tung-shan brought up this story: in behalf of Wu-cho
he held out his hand and said, "Leaving 'yes' and 'no' aside for the
moment, can I borrow this?"

Yao-shan and Ch'un Pu-na on washing Buddha   Ch'un Pu-
na was performing the ceremony of washing an icon of Buddha:
Yao-shan asked, "You may wash *this one*, but can you wash *that
one?*" Ch'un replied, "Bring me *that one.*" Yao-shan then stopped.

Yao-shan's saying on wearing a sword   As Yao-shan was
traveling in the mountains with Yun-yen, his sword rattled at his
side. Yun-yen said, "What's making that sound?" Yao-shan drew
his sword and made a cutting gesture. Later Tung-shan remarked
on this story, "See how Yao-shan lays himself down for this task; if
people of the present want to understand the transcendental, it is
necessary to understand the meaning of this first."

Further Readings

Scriptural Sources

T. Cleary. *Dhammapada: The Sayings of Buddha.* New York: Bantam Books, 1995

Buddhist Yoga: A Comprehensive Course. Boston: Shambhala Publications, 1995

The Flower Ornament Scripture. Boston: Shambhala Publications, 1993

Zen Works

T. Cleary. *Transmission of Light: Zen in the Art of Enlightenment.* Tokyo: Weatherhill, 1992

Zen Essence: The Science of Freedom. Boston: Shambhala Publications, 1989

Zen Lessons: The Art of Leadership. Boston: Shambhala Publications, 1988

T. & J.C. Cleary, *The Blue Cliff Record.* Boston: Shambhala Publications, 1977, 1992

Zen Letters: Teachings of Yuanwu. Boston: Shambhala Publications, 1994

J.C. Cleary, *Zen Dawn.* Boston: Shambhala Publications, 1996

Shambhala Dragon Editions

(Continued on next page)

Mastering the Art of War, by Zhuge Liang & Liu Ji. Translated & edited by Thomas Cleary.

The Myth of Freedom and the Way of Meditation, by Chögyam Trungpa.

Nine-Headed Dragon River, by Peter Matthiessen.

Rational Zen: The Mind of Dogen Zenji. Translated by Thomas Cleary.

Returning to Silence: Zen Practice in Daily Life, by Dainin Katagiri. Foreword by Robert Thurman.

Seeking the Heart of Wisdom: The Path of Insight Meditation, by Joseph Goldstein & Jack Kornfield. Foreword by H. H. the Dalai Lama.

Shambhala: The Sacred Path of the Warrior, by Chögyam Trungpa.

The Shambhala Dictionary of Buddhism and Zen.

The Spiritual Teaching of Ramana Maharshi, by Ramana Maharshi. Foreword by C. G. Jung.

Tao Teh Ching, by Lao Tzu. Translated by John C. H. Wu.

Teachings of the Buddha, Revised & Expanded Edition, edited by Jack Kornfield.

The Tibetan Book of the Dead: The Great Liberation through Hearing in the Bardo. Translated with commentary by Francesca Fremantle & Chögyam Trungpa.

Vitality, Energy, Spirit: A Taoist Sourcebook. Translated & edited by Thomas Cleary.

Wen-tzu: Understanding the Mysteries, by Lao-tzu. Translated by Thomas Cleary.

Worldly Wisdom: Confucian Teachings of the Ming Dynasty. Translated & edited by J. C. Cleary.

Zen Essence: The Science of Freedom. Translated & edited by Thomas Cleary.

The Zen Teachings of Master Lin-chi. Translated by Burton Watson.

Made in the USA
San Bernardino, CA
03 February 2014